Bloomsbury CPD Library: Stretch and Challenge

By Debbie Light

B L O O M S B U R Y

LONDON · OXFORD · NEW YORK · NEW DELHI · SYDNEY

Bloomsbury Education
An imprint of Bloomsbury Publishing Plc

50 Bedford Square	1385 Broadway
London	New York
WC1B 3DP	NY 10018
UK	USA

www.bloomsbury.com

Bloomsbury is a registered trademark of Bloomsbury Publishing Plc

First published 2017

British Library Cataloguing-in-Publication Data
A catalogue record for this book is available from the British Library.

ISBN:
PB: 9781472928405
ePub: 9781472928399
ePDF: 9781472928412

Library of Congress Cataloging-in-Publication Data
A catalog record for this book is available from the Library of Congress.

10 9 8 7 6 5 4 3 2 1

Typeset by Integra Software Services Pvt. Ltd.
Printed by CPI Group (UK) Ltd, Croydon, CR0 4YY

This book is produced using paper that is made from wood grown in
managed, sustainable forests. It is natural, renewable and recyclable.
The logging and manufacturing processes conform to the
environmental regulations of the country of origin.

To view more of our titles please visit www.bloomsbury.com

Contents

Acknowledgements

Thanks to my mum and dad for their continued support; I really couldn't have finished this book without their encouragement in what has been a difficult year. Huge thanks to my friend and colleague Stephen, who has been so kind and helpful whilst I've been writing the book. As always, sincere thanks to all my teacher friends who have shared their ideas and offered feedback over a glass of wine! Finally, none of this would have happened if it weren't for a very special teacher and friend, Mel, who left me to write this book on my own as she was off creating something else rather wonderful.

How to use this book

The Bloomsbury CPD Library provides primary and secondary teachers with affordable, comprehensive and accessible 'do-it-yourself' continuing professional development. This book focuses on stretching and challenging all of the students in your classroom.

The book is split into two halves: Part 1 **Teach yourself** and Part 2 **Train others**.

Teach yourself

This part of the book includes everything you need to improve your stretch and challenge practice. It is split into four stages:

STAGE 1: ASSESS

Stage 1 introduces the concept of stretch and challenge and why it is integral to excellent teaching and learning. In addition, there is a self-assessment questionnaire which will help you in reflecting on your current stretch and challenge practice as well as identify priority areas for development.

STAGE 2: IMPROVE

Stage 2 moves on to exploring the different approaches to planning excellent stretch and challenge provision. Linked to this, a range of key educational thinkers are introduced alongside a summary of their research into providing stretch and challenge for our students. This stage of the book ends with several case studies of teachers with different classes implementing new stretch and challenge approaches and strategies and reflecting on the impact they have on their students.

STAGE 3: EVALUATE

Stage 3 focuses on evaluating what steps you have taken to develop your approach to stretch and challenge; there is a self-assessment questionnaire to complete to support you in identifying how you have developed as a practitioner.

STAGE 4: EXCEL

Stage 4 looks at how you can continue to develop and embed your stretch and challenge practice and begin to influence the teaching and learning of your colleagues.

Train others

After completing Part 1 of the book, you will be ready to train others at your school and support them to develop their approach to stretch and challenge. Part 2 focuses on the role of the CPD leader and important areas to consider when preparing to train other colleagues. In-house CPD opportunities are becoming increasingly popular with schools as teachers realise how powerful in-house CPD can be when it is delivered by knowledgeable colleagues who can place training in the context of your school and your students.

There are training plans that can be adapted for all teachers to develop their stretch and challenge practice irrespective of how much time you have allocated to CPD at your school. Training plans include:

- A series of 15 minute briefings
- An INSET day
- A series of twilight sessions
- A lesson study programme

Don't forget to share how your training is going using #BloomsCPD!

Online resources

To download the templates, questionnaires and PowerPoints available for this book please visit www.bloomsbury.com/CPD-library-stretch-and-challenge.

Part 1

Teach yourself

1

What's it all about?

Stretch and challenge is the process of planning for learning to take place that will stretch all students to develop their knowledge and understanding, regardless of their starting points.

Stretch and challenge is a vital area of planning teaching and something every teacher should consider every time they plan a lesson. Regardless of the subject you teach, planning a lesson that caters for the needs of every student in front of you can be a tricky task. There are many factors to consider including:

- the age of the students in your class
- the ability of the students, their prior attainment and achievement data
- what you want your students to know by the end of the lesson
- what they are able to do based on what they have done previously
- what you expect of students in this particular class.

The hard part is creating an environment that allows all students to feel like they can reach their full potential, whatever their starting point.

The phrase 'full potential' brings up all sorts of issues: how do you really know what a student is capable of achieving in your classroom? As a starting point, most teachers will use some form of data to make a judgement about a student's ability, but this must only ever be a starting point. The job of the teacher is to use all they have at their disposal to push the student beyond what they think they are capable of – but this does not happen overnight! A classroom where stretch and challenge is truly valued and not seen as something that needs to be done to tick a box takes time to get right and is always evolving.

Getting it right

Teachers need to be committed to experimenting with different approaches in order to work out what is the best way forward for each student; the temptation to do what you've always done because it worked in the past needs to be resisted. Sure, there will be tried and tested approaches that will support students in meeting the challenges you set them, but reflective teachers will recognise that what they have in their teaching toolbox needs to be reconsidered and refined based on the profiles of new students they meet each year. It is also worth noting that any approach to stretch and challenge will struggle to be embedded into a teacher's normal planning if it is unmanageable. We all remember when we were trainees in this profession and only had to teach a few classes a week; it is common for trainees to spend hours producing differentiated materials but it quickly becomes apparent that this is not sustainable. Consequently, it is important to do a few things well rather than try every single approach if you really want to put stretch and challenge at the heart of your day-to-day planning.

Stretch and challenge vs differentiation: aren't they the same thing?

Well, no, not quite. Although they might sometimes take you to the same outcome, the spirit of them is different.

Stretch and challenge, as a concept, stemmed from the problems teachers found with differentiation. Differentiation often occurred due to teachers identifying a deficit in students; they can't do this, so I'll have to make up for this by producing something to help them. On the surface, there doesn't seem to be too much wrong with this but what this led to over time was a slow but steady dumbing down process. Too many differentiated worksheets, too many writing scaffolds, too many easier questions . . . before you know it, a student is completing lots of work and is being kept 'busy', but how much is their brain hurting? How used to struggling are they? Sometimes, differentiation can make learning too easy and if something is easy then students are not going to form a long-term memory.

Stretch and challenge sees possibilities rather than deficits. A teacher who has created an environment where stretch and challenge is encouraged will think that students are always capable of more than the students think they can do, if they are learning in the right conditions. It is the teacher's job to facilitate these conditions and push students to go beyond the limits they've imposed on themselves. It doesn't have to involve a multitude of different coloured worksheets or three versions of a writing frame; rather, the teacher invests time in diagnosing what the students can already do and working out how to move them onto the next challenge where it is a given that learning is hard work.

The keys to a successful stretch and challenge provision

There are myriad ways you can increase the challenge for your students and it can be daunting to know where to begin.

Know your students well

You can't stretch your students unless you really know what they are capable of – this goes beyond hard data! A student's data might show that they are a 'middle ability' student in your subject based on what they have achieved previously. However, that doesn't tell you the story behind that student. Do they like your subject? What are their gaps in learning? What are their strengths? Do they perform well in class but not in tests? Are they good at retaining information in their long-term memory?

These are just some of the questions you should be asking yourself when you are planning lessons. Where possible, try to be proactive rather than reactive; this way, you will have a head start on trying to get the best out of your students.

Stretch and challenge is not an add-on

Classrooms where great learning goes on often have one thing in common: you can feel the 'buzz' amongst the students because they enjoy being there and want to work hard. To create such a climate, it needs to become normal for students to know that they are going to work hard in your lesson; this may seem obvious, but students are very good at coasting and doing as little as possible if they can get away with it! Often we plan with the middle ability students in mind first – what do we expect most students in the class will be able to do? We then plan an activity to allow students to meet a particular learning objective. Our next thought is who might struggle to complete this activity successfully – we then create an easier resource to support that student. Finally, we might think about our accelerated learners who might finish that activity too quickly – an extension activity is created to keep them busy whilst the others are still working on the main activity. There's nothing inherently wrong with this way of lesson planning but unfortunately – whether you like it or not – you are making assumptions about students' abilities and putting a cap on what they can achieve at both ends of the ability scale. Instead, why not start with what you think your accelerated learners would be able to achieve and plan to support everyone in reaching that level.

All classes are mixed ability

Having taught in mixed ability groups and groups set by ability, I have experienced the pros and cons of both. There is a subconscious reaction that most teachers have if they teach in sets: teaching ability groups is easier because the range of ability is smaller, making it easier to pitch the lesson. While there is some truth in this claim, the trap that teachers can fall into is narrowing that ability range to such an extent that some students can get left behind. Just because you have two students in front of you who have a target level of a 6 (or a B grade in old money!) doesn't mean they will produce the same outcomes. It is still vital to diagnose what each student can and can't do and get beyond the data. If teaching a mixed ability group, it can seem overwhelming at first when confronted with such a wide range of ability but if you teach to the top and plan for those who may need extra support, it's amazing what some students will produce which is well beyond what the data told you they could do.

Never lower your expectations of what a student can do

Let's be honest: there are some classes that we all have in which it is a constant battle of wills. Similarly, there are classes which you might enjoy teaching during second period in the morning but when you teach them later in the week during fifth period, after lunch, they seem like a completely different class! The temptation when teaching classes or particular students who we find challenging, is to lower our expectations. We might not like to admit this but we are, after all, only human. The problem is that as soon as students get a whiff of you lowering your expectations, they will sit back and relax. Here's a classic example. Imagine you are teaching *Macbeth* to a low ability year 10 group. Do you study the full text with them, supplementing the reading with drama activities and scenes from different screen adaptations? Or do you watch the film first and then decide the bare minimum of scenes required to study in depth to 'get them through the exam'. I'm not pretending to be holier than thou here – I have fallen into the trap of choosing the second option in the past, but I was cheating my students out of some really interesting learning experiences. To put it bluntly, I put myself first and gave myself an easier life rather than put the effort into planning lessons that would have stretched the students, made them think hard and taken them out of their comfort zone. The lesson here is not to put a cap on what you think your students can do by the way you plan your lessons.

Involve your students by sharing your approaches with them

As soon as you decide that you are really going to value the process of stretch and challenge, it is not uncommon for some students to kick off: 'Why are you making us do this? Sir never made us do this before! Can't you just give us the correct answer? I told you already I'm not good at this.'

This is just one possible reaction you may have encountered when trying to get students to think hard and make their brains hurt – especially if they are not used to being challenged! However, once the initial shock of this exertion has worn off and students realise you are committed to creating a culture of high expectations, then most students want to do well. No student goes to school hoping they won't learn anything; normally, it's fear of failure that holds students back from pushing themselves that little bit harder during lessons. If you take the time to share your thinking with students and explain why you are using certain approaches, then it involves the students and they will be more willing to give things a go. Make time to talk to the students and ask them if what you're doing is helpful or is actually a hindrance; it is surprising how often we plough ahead without stopping to ask the students we are teaching if what we are doing is making a positive difference to them.

Increasing the challenge makes learning look messy

The 'progress debate' has been gathering pace recently; teachers are beginning to take a stand and say it is ridiculous to expect students to make progress that is both rapid and sustained. This fetish for rapid progress has led many teachers to plan easier learning tasks so that students look like they're making good progress. Who can blame teachers who fall into this trap when they might be observed by someone who can affect their pay; someone who may not have an understanding of the class context and who thinks the lesson has been a disaster because the students looked puzzled and weren't able to complete activities in a neat and orderly way. Thankfully, we are moving away from grading lessons and more and more school leaders are recognising that real learning takes time and can't be seen in one-off moments – that's just a showy performance. Real learning is a messy business; on one day students might seem like they've got it but the next week they may struggle again as you up the challenge. It is crucial that students know it is OK to fail, to struggle and to not always know the best way to proceed. These are all normal feelings that students will experience once you take them out of their comfort zone; without taking them out of their comfort zone, they cannot truly develop their knowledge and understanding and they cannot make great progress.

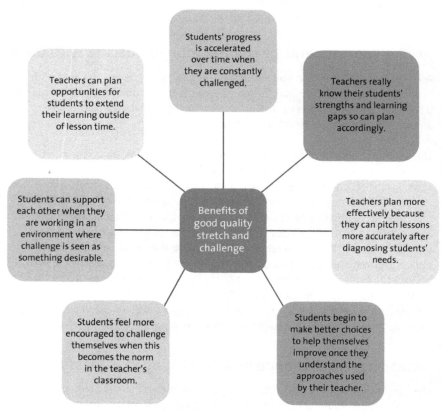

Fig. 1 Benefits of good-quality stretch and challenge

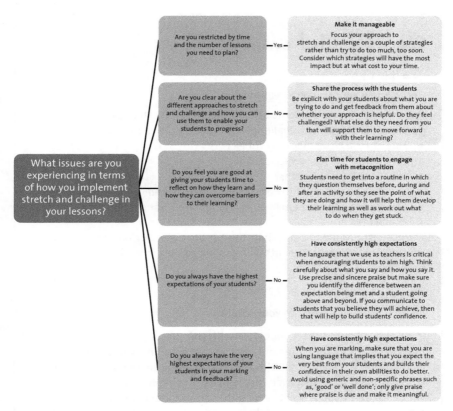

Fig. 2 What stretch and challenge action might be best for you right now?

Features of excellent stretch and challenge	Features of ineffective stretch and challenge
• Manageable	• Overambitious and time consuming
• Time built in to share and explain approaches with students	• Inadequate or no time given to share and explain approaches with students
• Time built in for students to reflect on how they are learning	• Students unaware of how they are learning or what progress they are making
• Well-organised and embedded into planning	• Disorganised and no embedding of approaches
• At the heart of lesson planning	• Does not inform planning; no refining of approaches
• Consistent high expectations	• Low or unclear expectations
• A common language used with students	• Language doesn't communicate high expectations.

Fig. 3 Features of excellent and ineffective approaches to stretch and challenge

Chapter 1 takeaway

Teaching tip

Get to know your students really well

Once you know your students beyond the data, you can begin to plan good-quality stretch and challenge. Questions to ask during planning are:

- How do they feel about my subject?
- What are their past experiences?
- What are their strengths?
- What do I want them to develop in the short, medium and long term?
- How can I support them in overcoming barriers and embracing challenge?

These questions are not an exhaustive list but a starting point to considering how your students will respond to the planned learning sequences.

Pass it on

Sharing your ideas – within your school

It is so important to share your ideas with your colleagues. As a rule, most of us don't like sharing our ideas in case we come across as foolish or, even worse, a know-it-all! However, the learning environment in your school could transform if every single teacher committed to sharing ideas with each other. You are all teaching the same students so what you are doing in your classroom might be incredibly helpful to a colleague in the next corridor. It is scary when you first start sharing things with colleagues if you haven't done so before, but it gets easier every time. Remember that it is the foot soldiers – the classroom teachers – that often have the answers rather than members of the senior leadership team (SLT) who will have a reduced teaching timetable. Newly-qualified teachers (NQTs) often have a lot of knowledge about current research but might not feel empowered to share it with more-experienced colleagues. Be brave and model to others what it means to be a thoughtful and reflective teacher. You can guarantee that what you have to say will be of some use to someone in your school.

You could, for example:

- Create pen portraits of students with whom you have tried particular approaches that have had a positive impact, and share them during a meeting or CPD session.

- Email around something you've tried with a class and ask others to try it too to see if it works for them.
- Put up on your teaching and learning noticeboard an interesting article, piece of research or blog you have read that might be useful to other colleagues.

Whatever approach you take, play your part in creating a stimulating and exciting learning culture amongst staff. This will, in turn, have a positive effect on students being taught by teachers at your school.

Share and tweet

Share your views on what you consider to be the point of stretch and challenge on Twitter using the hashtag #BloomsCPD.

CPD book club recommendation

Carol Dweck, *Mindset* (see Bibliography and further reading, page 271)

Bloggers' corner

Andy Tharby has some really good posts about stretch and challenge; check them out at: www.reflectingenglish.wordpress.com

---

TO DO LIST:

- ☐ Reflect on what you consider is good-quality stretch and challenge
- ☐ Reflect on your own approaches to stretch and challenge
- ☐ Tweet your reflections using the hashtag #BloomsCPD
- ☐ Share your thoughts and ideas with colleagues at your school
- ☐ Check out Andy Tharby's blog
- ☐ Read *Mindset* by Carol Dweck

2 Self-assessment

It is easy to just jump into trying something new as we all want to develop our practice, but if you want to see lasting impact, you need to choose wisely with regards to what aspects of your stretch and challenge provision you want to improve. It is crucial that you take some time to reflect on your current stretch and challenge provision; you may find that much of what you're doing is highly effective and you may only want to tweak one or two things. Or, stretch and challenge may be an area of pedagogy that you feel you need to put considerable work into developing and are ready to make some big changes to the way you challenge your students.

How to complete the self-evaluation questionnaire

On pages 18–29 there is a self-evaluation questionnaire to encourage you to start the 'teach yourself' process by thinking very carefully about the current stretch and challenge provision you provide in your classroom before you jump into trying to improve it.

When you are looking at your own stretch and challenge practices and trying to form a clear view of where you are now and what the next steps will be, there are many ways of approaching it – it will depend on you as a person. For some people, it is useful to go with your gut and listen to the first thing that comes into your mind – your instinctual answer. For others, it is a better approach to spend a good amount of time really mulling over the self-evaluation questions slowly and in detail. Whatever approach you decide to take, be honest with yourself about your current practice and remember that nobody will know the results of the questionnaire apart from you!

Quick response approach

If your preference for the self-evaluation is to go with your gut only, then simply fill in the quick response section after each question with the first thing that comes into your mind when you ask yourself the question. Do not mull over the question too long, simply read carefully and answer quickly. This approach will give you an overview of your current stretch and challenge understanding and practice and will take relatively little time. Just make sure you are uninterrupted, in a quiet place and able to complete the questionnaire in one sitting with no distractions so that you get focused and honest answers.

Considered response approach

If you choose to take a more reflective and detailed approach, then you can leave the quick response section blank and go straight onto reading the further guidance section under each question. This guidance provides prompt questions and ideas to get you thinking in detail about the question being asked and is designed to open up a wider scope in your answer. It will also enable you to look at your experience and pull examples into your answer to back up your statements. You may want to complete it a few questions at a time and take breaks, or you may be prepared to simply sit and work through the questions all in one sitting to ensure you remain focused. This approach does take longer, but it can lead to a more in-depth understanding of your current stretch and challenge practice, and you will gain much more from the process than the quick response alone.

Combined approach

A thorough approach, and one I recommend, would be to use both approaches together regardless of personal preference. There is clear value in both approaches being used together. This would involve you firstly answering the self-evaluation quick response questions by briefly noting down your instinctual answers for all

• I have done this self-assessment before. • I only want a surface level overview of my current understanding and practice. • I work better when I work at speed. • I don't have much time.	Quick
• I have never done this self-assessment before. • I want a deeper understanding of my current understanding and practice. • I work better when I take my time and really think things over. • I have some time to do this self-assessment.	Considered
• I have never done this self-assessment before. • I have done this self-assessment before. • I want a comprehensive and full understanding of my current understanding and practice and want to compare that to what I thought before taking the self-assessment. • I have a decent amount of time to dedicate to completing this self-assessment.	Combined

Fig. 4 How should I approach the self-evaluation questionnaire?

questions. The next step would be to return to the start of the self-evaluation, read the further guidance and then answer the questions once more, slowly and in detail forming more of a narrative around each question and pulling in examples from your own experience. Following this you would need to read over both responses and form a comprehensive and honest summary in your mind of your answers and a final view of where you feel you stand right now in your marking and feedback practice.

This is the longest of the three approaches to this questionnaire but will give you a comprehensive and full understanding of your current stretch and challenge practice. You will be surprised at the difference you see between the quick response and the considered response answers to the same questions. It can be very illuminating.

Rating	Definition
1	Not at all. I don't. None at all. Not happy. Not confident at all.
2	Rarely. Barely. Very little. Very unconfident.
3	Not often at all. Not much. Quite unconfident.
4	Not particularly. Not really. Not a lot. Mildly unconfident.
5	Neutral. Unsure. Don't know. Indifferent.
6	Sometimes. At times. Moderately. A little bit. Mildly confident.
7	Quite often. A fair bit. Some. A little confident.
8	Most of the time. More often than not. Quite a lot. Quite confident.
9	The majority of the time. A lot. Very confident.
10	Completely. Very much so. A huge amount. Extremely happy. Extremely confident.

Fig. 5 Rate yourself definitions

Rate yourself

The final part of the self-evaluation is to rate yourself. This section will ask you to rate your confidence and happiness in each area that has been covered in the questionnaire, with a view to working on these areas for improvement throughout the course of the book. The table below shows how the scale works: the higher the number you allocate yourself, the better you feel you are performing in that area.

Top tip

It would be easy to rush through this questionnaire or skip it altogether – often, we're looking for quick wins to improve our teaching, the magic bullet that will transform our practice. However, if you really want to make long-term gains, then it's imperative that you make time to consider how you are planning and delivering lessons before deciding on any changes to your current practice. Be honest about your strengths and weaknesses but, at the same time, be kind to yourself: we are often our harshest critics! Where you feel there is an area that you need to work on, be constructive in the criticism you give to yourself; what could you realistically change that you could incorporate into your routine planning? Finally, when completing this questionnaire, consider all of the classes you teach – don't shy away from your toughest classes as this could be where you could make the biggest difference in refining your approach to stretch and challenge.

Stretch and challenge self-evaluation questionnaire

QUESTION 1: Do you enjoy planning stretch and challenge opportunities?

Quick response:

_____

_____

_____

_____

Questions for consideration

- What do you like about lesson planning?
- Do you think first about planning activities or planning learning outcomes?
- What types of approaches do you most routinely use to stretch and challenge your students?

Considered response:

_____

_____

_____

_____

_____

_____

_____

_____

_____

_____

Rate yourself

QUESTION 1: How much do you enjoy planning stretch and challenge opportunities?

1   2   3   4   5   6   7   8   9   10

QUESTION 2: What do you think makes effective stretch and challenge?

Quick response:

_____

_____

_____

_____

Questions for consideration

- Do you approach stretch and challenge in the same way with all of your classes?
- Are you organised and have you embedded routines into your classroom?
- Do you know why you favour certain approaches and is there evidence they are the best approaches to use?

Considered response:

_____

_____

_____

_____

_____

_____

_____

_____

_____

_____

_____

_____

_____

Rate yourself

QUESTION 2: How happy are you with your approach to stretch and challenge at the moment?

1   2   3   4   5   6   7   8   9   10

QUESTION 3: Where do you feel your strengths lie with stretch and challenge?

Quick response:

_____

_____

_____

_____

Questions for consideration

- What do you feel you do well?
- How have your approaches developed over time?
- Are there any elements of your approach to stretch and challenge that have been acknowledged and praised by colleagues, students or parents?

Considered response:

_____

_____

_____

_____

_____

_____

_____

_____

_____

_____

_____

Rate yourself

QUESTION 3: How confident do you feel when it comes to your approach to stretch and challenge?

| 1 | 2 | 3 | 4 | 5 | 6 | 7 | 8 | 9 | 10 |

QUESTION 4: Where do you feel your weaknesses lie with stretch and challenge?

Quick response:

_____

_____

_____

_____

Questions for consideration

- What do you think are your priorities for developing your approach to stretch and challenge?
- Have you always struggled with these aspects of stretch and challenge?
- Has any support been offered to help you develop your practice or have you undertaken training or wider reading to improve?

Considered response:

_____

_____

_____

_____

_____

_____

_____

_____

_____

_____

_____

Rate yourself

QUESTION 4: How serious do you think your weaknesses are when it comes to your approach to stretch and challenge?

1   2   3   4   5   6   7   8   9   10

QUESTION 5: What data do you use to plan effective stretch and challenge?

Quick response:

_____

_____

_____

_____

Questions for consideration

- How do you make use of summative data?
- How do you make use of formative data?
- What examples can you think of in which you have retaught something or refined the way you have taught something based on what has been revealed by analysing students' data?

Considered response:

_____

_____

_____

_____

_____

_____

_____

_____

_____

_____

_____

_____

Rate yourself

QUESTION 5: How confident are you that you are using a range of data to plan effective stretch and challenge?

1   2   3   4   5   6   7   8   9   10

QUESTION 6: Do you feel your approach to stretch and challenge has impact upon student attainment and achievement in your classroom?

Quick response:

_____

_____

_____

_____

Questions for consideration

- When have you seen direct impact after implementing a particular stretch and challenge approach?
- Why do you think this approach was successful?
- What examples can you think of where individual students have been able to move forward and make progress?

Considered response:

_____

_____

_____

_____

_____

_____

_____

_____

_____

_____

_____

Rate yourself

QUESTION 6: How much impact on student attainment and achievement do you feel your approach to stretch and challenge has at the moment?

1	2	3	4	5	6	7	8	9	10

QUESTION 7: What educational research, theories or case studies about stretch and challenge do you know about that informs or influences your practice?

Quick response:

_____

_____

_____

_____

Questions for consideration

- How do you access educational research?
- Have you conducted any of your own research with your classes and was it a valuable experience?
- Have you discussed any findings from academic research with your colleagues?

Considered response:

_____

_____

_____

_____

_____

_____

_____

_____

_____

_____

Rate yourself

QUESTION 7: How confident are you in your knowledge of educational research into approaches to stretch and challenge?

1	2	3	4	5	6	7	8	9	10

QUESTION 8: Is there anything that is holding you back in developing your approach to stretch and challenge?

Quick response:

_____

_____

_____

_____

Questions for consideration

- What do you find difficult about planning good-quality stretch and challenge?
- Is there anything you've tried to overcome time and time again but have not got quite right?
- What constraints do you feel you have placed upon you when it comes to planning effective stretch and challenge?

Considered response:

_____

_____

_____

_____

_____

_____

_____

_____

_____

_____

_____

Rate yourself

QUESTION 8: How much are these things holding you back in terms of improving your approach to stretch and challenge?

| 1 | 2 | 3 | 4 | 5 | 6 | 7 | 8 | 9 | 10 |

QUESTION 9: Do you feel your views on effective stretch and challenge match those of the school you work in?

Quick response:

_____

_____

_____

_____

Questions for consideration

- Does your school have a whole-school approach to stretch and challenge, or is there freedom for teachers to plan in any way they feel works for their students?
- Is there anything about your school's approach that you feel does not work for you? If so, why?
- How do you feel students and parents think about the way your school tries to stretch and challenge students?

Considered response:

_____

_____

_____

_____

_____

_____

_____

_____

_____

_____

Rate yourself

QUESTION 9: How closely do you feel yours and your school's views on effective stretch and challenge align?

1   2   3   4   5   6   7   8   9   10

QUESTION 10: Do you feel your views on stretch and challenge match those of the department you work in?

Quick response:

_____

_____

_____

_____

Questions for consideration

- Do you feel that your department's approach is in line with what you consider to be important with regards to good-quality stretch and challenge?
- What do you feel your department does well and not so well with regards to good-quality stretch and challenge?
- If you could design an effective departmental approach to stretch and challenge, what would it look like?

Considered response:

_____

_____

_____

_____

_____

_____

_____

_____

_____

_____

_____

Rate yourself

QUESTION 10: How closely do you feel yours and your department's views on effective stretch and challenge align?

1	2	3	4	5	6	7	8	9	10

QUESTION 11: Do you have an accurate understanding of what your colleagues think about your approach to stretch and challenge?

Quick response:

_____
_____
_____
_____

Questions for consideration

- Have you ever spoken to colleagues about your approach to stretch and challenge?
- Have you ever had any feedback from your head of department or other senior staff following lesson observations or book looks?
- Have you ever adapted anything about your approach to stretch and challenge based on conversations with colleagues?

Considered response:

_____
_____
_____
_____
_____
_____
_____
_____
_____

Rate yourself

QUESTION 11: How confident are you that you know what colleagues think about your approach to stretch and challenge?

| 1 | 2 | 3 | 4 | 5 | 6 | 7 | 8 | 9 | 10 |

QUESTION 12: What do your students think about how you plan opportunities for them to be suitably challenged?

Quick response:

_____

_____

_____

_____

Questions for consideration

- Have you ever spoken to your students about the lessons you have planned for them?
- Have you ever adapted anything in response to feedback from your students?
- Do your students understand your approach to challenging them or are they unaware of your approach?

Considered response:

_____

_____

_____

_____

_____

_____

_____

_____

_____

_____

Rate yourself

QUESTION 12: How confident are you that you really know what students feel and think about how you plan opportunities for them to be suitably challenged?

| 1 | 2 | 3 | 4 | 5 | 6 | 7 | 8 | 9 | 10 |

The results

Well done, you have self-evaluated your stretch and challenge practice and are now a step forward in the right direction to becoming an expert in creating high-challenge learning environments! You have considered your current approaches and whether they are leading to improved student outcomes; how confident and knowledgeable you are in the latest research about how to stretch and challenge students; whether your approach or approaches you'd like to try are aligned to the ideologies of your department and the wider school; how you communicate your approach to students, parents and other colleagues across school. It is a lot to consider so give yourself sufficient time to reflect on your self-evaluation before making any decisions.

Take a look at how you rated your answers for each question in the questionnaire and compare your ratings with the chart below which will guide you to taking the next steps in your stretch and challenge practice.

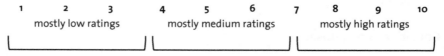

Fig. 6 How did you rate yourself?

Mostly low ratings

You have some way to go before you feel confident that the approaches you are using are having maximum impact on students' achievement. However, this is the start of something really exciting as you are going to be in the position to try various approaches and critically reflect on the impact these are having on your students. Decide now on your first priority that you want to work on based on the responses to the questions. Remember that making any sustained improvement takes time so ensure you commit to giving your new approach time to embed.

Mostly medium ratings

You have some experience in providing stretch and challenge for your students that is having some impact but there are still areas that you need to give greater thought to if you are to push your students to accelerate their learning. Consider all the possible areas you could focus on and decide which ones you want to prioritise and that you can commit to realistically. It is better to focus on one or two areas and master these rather than try and take on too much.

Mostly high ratings

You are confident in your approach to proving effective stretch and challenge. You have already carried out wider reading around this area of pedagogy and can justify the approaches you have decided to use with your students. However, reflective practitioners are always looking to improve and make further marginal gains with their students and you will be no different! At this point, you may want to refine small areas of your practice and begin to consider supporting other colleagues through providing training on how to develop stretch and challenge. Although you are highly effective, always keep your eyes and ears open so that you can be responsive to new ideas that other colleagues are keen to share with you.

Now what?

You've completed your questionnaire and have looked closely at your responses to each question, which will highlight particular strengths and weaknesses that you have with regards to your stretch and challenge provision. Spend time drawing up an action plan for working towards mastering this area of pedagogy. Set yourself short-, medium- and long-term goals and be clear with yourself about what impact you want to see so you can judge the effectiveness of approach going forward.

Chapter 2 takeaway

Teaching tip
Don't try and change too much, too soon
How many times have you come back from a course and felt reenergised and vowed to implement all that you've heard from the speaker? We're all guilty of getting excited about trying something new but rarely do we embed these new ideas into our daily practice. After you've completed your questionnaire, give it a few days before returning to your answers. Let the results sink in before prioritising what you should begin to do differently or what you should keep doing that is working well already. Narrow down your focus so that you only take on one or two areas to work on.

Pass it on
Sharing your ideas – why it's good to share
Once you have committed to developing your practice, it is natural that you will reflect more on your practice, carry out some wider reading into stretch and challenge and begin to experiment with some new strategies. If you share what you're doing with other colleagues, then it

is more likely you will keep focused on what it is you're trying to improve. Colleagues might pose questions that you haven't thought of or might be shying away from; get their input and be open to discussion. It might be a good idea to share the results of your questionnaire with your team and encourage them to complete it; this should stimulate a fruitful discussion on how you and the team can move forward and plan for more effective stretch and challenge.

Also, it's only fair to share your successes with other colleagues so that more students can benefit from effective approaches. You might prefer to speak to colleagues face-to-face in the staffroom, or you may make a more formal contribution during CPD sessions and meetings. Alternatively, you might feel more comfortable emailing colleagues or sharing a link to a website or blog that discusses something you've been trying out with your students. The manner in which you choose to share your ideas doesn't matter – so be brave and play your part in creating a culture in which colleagues enjoy talking about pedagogy.

Share and tweet
Share your views about what you have found interesting after completing the questionnaire on Twitter using the hashtag #BloomsCPD.

CPD book club recommendations
Ron Berger, *An Ethic of Excellence*
(see Bibliography and further reading, page 271)

Bloggers' corner
Tom Sherrington has some excellent posts on effective stretch and challenge and his blog is well worth a read. Visit his blog at: www.headguruteacher.com.

TO DO LIST:

☐ Share the results of your self-assessment questionnaire with your colleagues
☐ Share what you have learned about your stretch and challenge practice using the hashtag #BloomsCPD
☐ Read Tom Sherrington's blog at www.headguruteacher.com
☐ Read Ron Berger's *An Ethic of Excellence*

3 Approaches to stretch and challenge

There is no one approach to stretch and challenge that will be the magic bullet for suddenly challenging all of your students and them making excellent progress; there are many approaches and each one has its advantages and disadvantages. Before deciding to change any aspect of your practice, consider what the issues might be in your classroom. Is there a general feeling of lethargy with one class or is it just one group of students which isn't really showing any signs of quality learning? Are the issues something you think can be overcome quite easily or is the issue so deep-rooted that it could take several lessons before seeing any positive change?

The students

Whichever approach you choose to incorporate into your practice, it is best – where possible – to share as much information with your students as you can, so they understand why you are trying something new. Clearly, this could be a sensitive process if it involves only a couple of students; you don't want to single any one out and make them feel embarrassed. However, you also don't want to send out the wrong message and seem to be accepting low standards, which is why it is so important to be honest with students about what it is you are trying to achieve and how you think you might be able to support them in stretching themselves to achieve better.

As mentioned in my takeaway tip in the last chapter (page 31), be careful not to overload your students with a whole new array of strategies and approaches. If you change too much too soon, you might encounter a class full of puzzled faces. Decide on one or two approaches to experiment with and see what response you get from your students.

Lesson planning

Below I have outlined a number of approaches to stretch and challenge, focusing on different aspects of lesson planning. Whatever stage you are in your teaching career, have a look at the different approaches to stretch and challenge that a teacher could use with their classes; some may be new to you or it may be a case of reminding yourself about them. Are there any approaches that you may have used in the past but haven't used for a while? Teachers are known for forgetting what they have in their teaching toolbox and relying on a small number of approaches because they feel comfortable with them.

Finally, no approach will work for everyone. You might feel that a particular approach is most suited to a small group of students or perhaps might work better with older students. To become better at anything, trial and error is part of the process so make sure you give yourself enough time to see what impact these approaches may have with all of the classes you teach.

Learning intentions

Overview:

There is much controversy surrounding learning outcomes and how best to share learning intentions with students. Should they write them down? Should you share them at the beginning of the lesson or after some sort of 'hook' task? It is crucial that students understand what they are supposed to be learning and that the teacher shares the learning journey with them – otherwise, students focus on just doing activities without understanding how these activities actually develop their learning.

Why this approach could be useful:

Spending time on your approach to sharing learning intentions can support all of the class in aiming high. Think carefully about how you word your learning intentions to explicitly convey to the students that there is a clear level of challenge in what you expect them to learn. You may have the same learning intentions over a series of lessons if what you want them to learn is particularly challenging; the important thing is to frame the learning journey as something challenging with clear progression. Structure of learning outcomes (SOLO taxonomy) is one way that the teacher can frame learning intentions that become progressively more challenging without using the dreaded 'All, must, some' of the past.

Issues to consider:

There's no getting away from the fact that spending time covering learning intentions does eat into lesson time, so think carefully about how long you are going to give over to this part of the lesson. Are you just reeling off learning intentions without really getting students to engage with the learning process? Breaking up the sharing of learning intentions by posing questions to the students to ensure they have understood how the learning intentions are becoming more challenging, is important to stop this part of the lesson from being a waste of time.

When you might use it:

At the starts of lessons, you might want to share your learning intentions visually in combination with a 'hook' task to help the students understand what they are going to be learning. If you do not want to spend too much time on visually sharing your learning intentions and discussing the learning journey as you have a lot of content to cover, you might decide to create some larger learning intentions for the topic that you share at the beginning and refer back to at several points during the topic rather than every lesson.

Benefit for students:

You can really get students to engage well with challenging learning intentions if you embed the process into your own classroom routines and encourage the students to aim high in what they can achieve. Depending on the class, there may be some student choice over what they think they can achieve or you may have to use a more direct approach if particular students are coasting or lacking confidence.

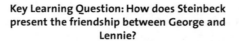

Key Learning Question: How does Steinbeck present the friendship between George and Lennie?

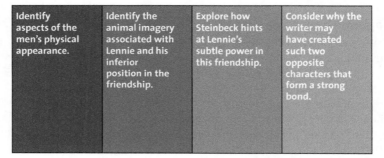

| Identify aspects of the men's physical appearance. | Identify the animal imagery associated with Lennie and his inferior position in the friendship. | Explore how Steinbeck hints at Lennie's subtle power in this friendship. | Consider why the writer may have created such two opposite characters that form a strong bond. |

Fig. 7 Example of sharing learning intentions which have a clear level of challenge, adapted from SOLO taxonomy

Independence and resilience

Overview:

A key aspect of stretch and challenge is creating the right conditions to support all students to be able to work independently, but this takes time and a great deal of effort. We can't expect students to be able to just go off and learn successfully by themselves if they do not have quality teacher input to begin with. Yet I don't know of any teacher who feels like they wouldn't like their students to build their resilience. The problem with increasing the level of challenge and what you expect of students is that some of them will struggle, and they don't like that feeling of being out of their depth; however, if they don't experience that struggle then they can't improve. Helping students to feel familiar with struggling is an important role the teacher has when planning for student progress.

Why this approach might be useful:

Getting students used to being challenged is one of the most important things you can do as a teacher and really proves to students that you have high expectations of them all. Explicitly sharing with students that you want them to struggle and for them to do something with less input from you will seem strange and discomforting to some students – in particular, those who have benefited from a lot of teacher or teaching assistant (TA) input in the past. A relatively easy way to help those students you've identified as needing to improve their resilience, is to chunk the task into smaller achievable goals that students can tick off as they go; often, students feel like they can't do something because the task seems overwhelming if the teacher isn't going to help them. Invest time in creating some task checklists as a support for students to become more resilient and independent.

Issues to consider:

Be prepared for a possible change in behaviour from some students when you up the level of challenge in this way. They may be used to having a lot of work done for them and won't know how to react. Initially, some students may disengage with learning for fear of looking stupid; others might play up and display some silly behaviour. All of this is to be expected. If the teacher can overlook some of these initial negative learning behaviours, focus on any positive reactions to this increase in challenge and give sincere praise when students achieve something they haven't achieved before by themselves, then slowly students will begin to learn that they need to show some resilience if they are to develop their learning.

When you might use it:

This approach works best with a small group of students rather than a whole class. Although you could use this approach with a whole class, you might find that you are run ragged by lots of students saying they can't do something or a number of students going off task quickly once they lose interest and don't have you to do the work for them. Rather, it might be best to decide which students in particular will assume that you will do a lot of the work for them. Start first with these students and introduce the task checklist. You might find you have to monitor how they get on with this different approach to accomplishing a task and you won't be able to monitor their reaction if you need to watch the whole class.

Benefit for students:

Once students get used to being challenged and see it as the norm that they will have to struggle by themselves and can't rely on the teacher to do things for them, then each time they learn something new it will get easier.

A big benefit to this approach is that students will feel a sense of pride in accomplishing a task by themselves. If students do persist in asking for your help rather than struggling alone, set a timer and get them to try by themselves for five minutes before you give any input. Alternatively, you could give them a set number of questions they can ask during a task – encourage them not to use them up too quickly.

Task: To write an analysis of George and Lennie's friendship in *Of Mice and Men*.

Step 1: Read the extract and highlight four quotations that focus on their friendship. ☐

Step 2: Look at your quotations and decide if they show something positive or negative about their friendship. ☐

Step 3: Look at your quotations and decide on the most interesting word or phrase from each one. Circle it. ☐

Step 4: Look at the words you have circled. What do they make you think or feel? Jot down those thoughts in the margin. ☐

Step 5: Use your Reading Ladder to help you write a paragraph for your first quotation. ☐

Step 6: Write three more paragraphs. ☐

Step 7: Read your answer over and check that you have included the key words from our key word box. ☐

Have you included the following key words?

Migrant workers
Great Depression
Dust Bowl
American Dream
Reliance
Dominance
Loneliness

Fig. 8 Example of developing independence by using checklists

Questioning and discussion

Overview:

Thinking about the questions you want to ask your students as well as questions you would like students to ask each other is a really vital form of stretch and challenge. Great questioning leads to great thinking. Often, if we're short of time, we might think about the questions we ask students at that moment in class; unfortunately, this often leads to the questions not being challenging enough and the same students dominating as a result of no thought being put into who to direct the questions to during the lesson. Setting aside a few minutes to think about how you will use questions and encourage students to create their own to provoke thinking will be a great use of planning time.

Why this approach might be useful:

One form of questioning and discussion that tends to dominate classrooms is the IRF model (initiate a question, listen to a student's response, give feedback on whether the response is right or wrong). The teacher initiates a question, the student or students respond and the teacher gives feedback on whether the response was correct before moving on. There is nothing inherently wrong with this, but if this is the only method of questioning you use, then some students will be losing out. More than likely you have students in your class who would never dream of answering questions unless they were forced into doing so. The IRF model won't work for them because they're under no pressure to respond. Effective questioning is a non-negotiable of stretch and challenge provision. A well-structured question can reveal a student's thinking as well as set off other questions in the student's mind. Effective questioning doesn't require a huge amount of resourcing; instead, the teacher will need to spend time thinking about the types of questions to pose, who to pose them to and when to use them during the lesson.

Issues to consider:

Although it is a good idea to plan your questions in advance, there will be times when your lesson goes off on an unexpected tangent and this is no bad thing. Definitely plan a few questions you know you want to ask the students to help them move forward with their knowledge and understanding, but also give some time to other questions that crop up that you haven't thought of – these can be some of the best questions! Another issue to consider is that some students will feel uncomfortable talking at length, even in front of just one student. Think very carefully about how you pair or group students together for a question-led task. If the dynamics aren't right, then you may not get much out of particular students – although the structured approach of a Socratic discussion (see chapter 4, page 60) should help to overcome those awkward silences.

When you might use it:

If you feel you've got yourself into a bit of a questioning rut and the same students keep answering all your questions, this might be a good approach to explore as it increases student participation and develops their thinking. Any topic you are teaching that requires students to think of different possibilities or think beyond a superficial level will benefit from good-quality questioning and opportunities for discussion.

Benefit for students:

Most students will appreciate the chance to talk but might not be equipped with the tools to do so effectively. A great way to stretch students is to get them thinking really hard, and well-structured discussion can provide a means of helping them do so. Stretch and challenge through questioning will work in low-achieving groups who may be reluctant to speak out or high-achieving groups who are struggling to go beyond the obvious in their response to questioning.

Question: Is George a good friend to Lennie?

Conceptual Clarification
- How does this question relate to what we have just read?
- Can you give me an example of George being a good friend to Lennie?

Probing Assumptions
- What else have we read that might prove that George is a good friend to Lennie?
- Is there anything else you've read that might show George in a different light?

Probing reasons
- How might some readers think that George is not a good friend?
- What evidence is there in the novel to make this counterargument?

Questioning perspectives
- What alternative ways are there of looking at George and Lennie's relationship, other than just being friends?
- How might this be a more useful way of looking at these characters?

Probing consequences
- Why is this question so important for our reading of this novel?
- Taking everything into account, which interpretation may be the most useful one?

Fig. 9 Example of challenging students through questioning and discussion using Socratic discussion

Choice of task

Overview:

Having a selection of tasks can be a useful way to support all students in accessing the learning but there can be pitfalls to this way of stretching the class if it is not carefully thought through when planning. The teacher wants to ensure that the task is pitched at the right level so that there is an appropriate amount of challenge for all. One thing to consider is how much choice the students will have: will they have totally free reign to pick any task or will you direct the students to appropriate tasks? Another thing to take into consideration is not to put a ceiling on what you think the student can achieve; a way of avoiding this would be to let students know the range of tasks available so they can stretch themselves further if they begin on a task which they find relatively easy to complete.

Why this approach might be useful:

Sometimes, when one main task is set for all students to tackle, some students can get left behind and complete only some of it; others may complete the task early and then be given extension work. This extension work is often more of the same so there is not always an increase in challenge. Planning a range of tasks gives you options as a teacher. Once you have clearly defined and shared why some of the tasks might be more challenging than others, you could decide to get the class to work through a series of tasks at their own pace. Or you may have students starting at different points based on their prior learning. If you encourage all students to start with the most difficult task and not waste time with the easier tasks, students can always drop down to the slightly easier task if the level of challenge is beyond their reach.

Issues to consider:

Unless you visually display the range of tasks available, then students may stick to just one task and not push themselves to attempt the most challenging tasks. Or you may have students who misjudge where they are with their learning and select an inappropriate task – it is the teacher's job to work with the students to make good task choices. Once students get used to having some level of choice, they become better at making good task choices but will most likely need guidance in the early stages. Finally, a note of caution: this approach does not mean making ten different versions of a worksheet or dumbing down the learning process! It is more focused on choosing a really challenging task and then making small tweaks to the task to ensure everyone has a fair shot at trying to access the learning.

When you might use it:

This approach is well-suited to a mixed-ability class with varying levels of achievement; however, it can also be used in classes grouped by similar levels of attainment if students are guilty of coasting and need an extra challenge rather than a 'more of the same' extension approach. Displaying all the tasks for students to see also encourages students to think about their progress and where they are in their learning journey. It requires students to make good judgements and become more active with their learning.

Benefit for students:

An increased level of autonomy is a significant plus for this approach to stretch and challenge if it is carefully used by teachers. There is also flexibility with this approach as students can start at different points which are right for them. The staggered increase in level of challenge will also seem much more obtainable to those students who may lack confidence in tackling a really challenging task straight away.

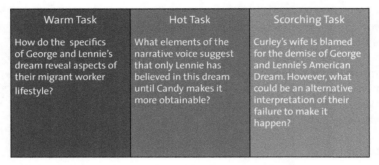

Key Learning Question: How does Steinbeck present the concept of the American Dream?

Warm Task	Hot Task	Scorching Task
How do the specifics of George and Lennie's dream reveal aspects of their migrant worker lifestyle?	What elements of the narrative voice suggest that only Lennie has believed in this dream until Candy makes it more obtainable?	Curley's wife Is blamed for the demise of George and Lennie's American Dream. However, what could be an alternative interpretation of their failure to make it happen?

Fig. 10 Example of stretching students by providing a choice of tasks

Resources

Overview:

An alternative to planning different tasks is to plan only one task but have a selection of resources to support students in accessing the learning. When planning a task, consider what aspects of the task particular students in your class will struggle with and then consider what type of resource may be useful to help them meet the challenge. Resources that could support students' learning are: sentence stems; a prompt; access to a textbook; a series of thinking questions; a glossary; a set of instructions; visuals; a YouTube clip if there is access to the Internet.

Why this approach might be useful:

There will be times when you need everyone in the class to all work on the same task, for example, when planning for a practical or a piece of extended writing. Yet, the teacher will know that not everyone will be able to do the task individually without some sort of input and this is why this approach to stretch and challenge is particularly useful. All students will be expected to aim high and meet the learning challenge but will take different routes to get there.

Issues to consider:

Some students can end up relying on your resources even when they don't really need them any more – think of it as a comfort blanket. If a student is always used to completing a certain type of task using a particular resource, then they will be reluctant to try without any support. It's the teacher's job to acknowledge this and encourage the student to attempt a task without using the resource. Linked to this, the teacher may feel that the student still needs to use the resource to access the task but may want to make the student wait before using it to build up their resilience. This approach will only work if the teacher is clear on who needs what and when they might need to use it.

When you might use it:

This approach works best when a student is attempting something out of their comfort zone and will produce a piece of work which is substantial enough to receive feedback. You want them to produce something of quality but may be aware that they are not quite ready to complete the task by themselves. Rather than dumb down the task, the teacher is able to keep the level of challenge high but supplement it with useful support resources.

Benefit for students:

This is an approach that allows students to take more responsibility for their learning and to make decisions about what support they need to complete tasks. Moreover, as everyone is attempting the same task, it encourages low-achieving students to take a risk and complete work that their high-achieving peers are doing; sometimes just raising your expectations of students in this way can lead to improved outcomes.

In addition to the Key Words and Paragraph Starters in the figure below, students were provided with images under the heading of 'What do we know about the context of the novel?' See the online resources for this example.

Essay title: How does Steinbeck present the theme of loneliness in the novel?	
Key Words	**Paragraph Starters**
Isolation Migrant workers Competitive Companionship Mistrust Prejudice	In the novel, Steinbeck uses the friendship between George and Lennie to highlight... Steinbeck uses the relationship between Candy and his dog to explore... Crooks experiences loneliness in the novel due to... The novel's ending is symbolic of the harsh reality of 1930s America as Lennie's death represents...

Fig. 11 Example of a resource to support students in writing an essay

Groupings

Overview:

Nothing gets teachers arguing more than the phrase 'group work'. Some advocate as much group work as possible, arguing that students should be given opportunities to collaborate and learn from their peers; others see group work as a waste of precious learning time and believe students see it as a social activity, quickly going off-task. Regardless of these differing positions, there are times when students working collaboratively is an excellent way to raise the level of challenge.

Why this approach might be useful:

Although there are times when students need to work individually and show what they can produce without anyone else's input, collaborative working can support students in developing their knowledge and understanding – as long as it is set up properly. The key to this approach of working is flexibility: different types of groupings will bring about different outcomes. The teacher needs to know the strengths and weaknesses of the students and group students accordingly and students can learn from each other and develop their thinking by sharing, listening and refining their initial thoughts. Group roles should be assigned so that all students are pulling their weight and not relying on one or two students to do all the work. Roles can be assigned for a whole topic so students learn how to become an expert in one particular area, or the teacher can assign different roles to give students a range of learning experiences.

Issues to consider:

Think really carefully about why working in groups would be more beneficial than students working individually. Group work can be an absolute nightmare to begin with; you must invest time in training students how to work effectively and be clear in your expectations of what each student is bringing to the task. If your desire for them to work collaboratively is purely social, then this might not be enough reason to spend time doing group work. The level of cognitive challenge needs to be strong enough to warrant collaboration where everyone in the group can be held to account for their contributions.

When you might use it:

There are two types of groupings you can use – groups with similar levels of attainment and groups which have mixed attainment. If you are introducing students to a new, challenging concept where they have to produce something specific as an outcome, then groups of similar ability may be best so students will be working at a similar cognitive level. However, if the task is more open-ended where students' understanding will be enhanced by diverse opinions and ideas, a mixed attainment group could work.

Benefit for students:

The more students know, the more connections they can make, the more their understanding increases. One way of increasing students' knowledge is to get them to work with others to learn from each other. If students get into good working habits over time where they support each other, encourage each other to develop their thinking and rely less on the teacher to spoon feed them, the benefits to their learning are significant.

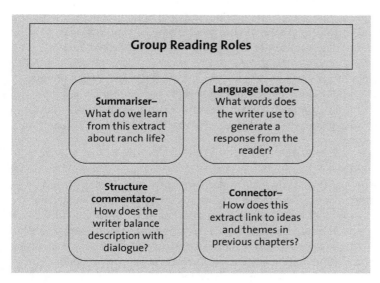

Fig. 12 Example of group roles to challenge students to participate effectively in a task

Feedback

Overview:

Feedback is the most important thing a student receives from the teacher as it helps to close the learning gaps. Feedback should be regular and timely and the teacher needs to monitor that the students are putting into practice what the feedback has suggested they work on. A key way to stretch students is the way in which you set up feedback processes with your class. There are myriad ways of giving students feedback but it is equally important to think about how you are setting up a culture in which students want to receive feedback from the teacher and their peers because they recognise that the more open they are to receiving feedback, the more they will develop as learners. Therefore, time should be set aside to get students into a routine of sharing work, asking for feedback and making changes based on the feedback they are given.

Why this approach might be useful:

Teachers can often despair at how much effort they put into assessing students' work and how little students seem to get out of it. If a teacher is spending hours giving feedback then we need to make sure that students are working equally hard responding to our feedback and closing their learning gaps. Setting up a culture of critique in your class goes beyond traditional notions of assessment; in a class where a culture of critique is clearly established, the process is so embedded that students naturally seek feedback and want to work harder to improve their work. Students recognise that their work can be improved and that their first attempt at a piece of work is not going to be the best they can produce. One way in which this culture of critique can become part of your classes is by using the gallery technique, displaying students' work so everyone in the class gets a chance to share their work and receive feedback from multiple students as well as their teacher.

Issues to consider:

If students are not used to having their work commented on and being offered constructive criticism, then this can feel very daunting. 'What if other students or my teacher think my work is rubbish?' is a common question from less confident students when you introduce this new way of critiquing each other's work. In order for a culture of critique to be successful, the teacher must have very clear guidelines that are visible at all times during any feedback process to support students; clear success criteria needs to be shared with the students so that any comments can be directly related to the quality of their work as opposed to ego-driven feedback. The teacher should also model to their students how to give feedback by sharing good and bad feedback practices and asking students to identify what makes effective feedback so that the role of feedback is not just the teacher's but also so that the students are involved in understanding what quality work looks like.

When you might use it:

The teacher needs to decide in advance which tasks in the topic are going to be assessed and warrant a considerable amount of time being spent on them. Once these tasks have been identified, then the teacher can share this information with their students so they know their work is going to be assessed and critiqued. Knowing that their work is going to be seen as important should give students an extra motivation to produce their best work. Sometimes this approach is useful when you want to get students to attempt a task at the beginning of the topic and then try something similar later in the topic so that they get a sense of how their knowledge and understanding is developing over time.

Benefit for students:

This stretch and challenge approach can be used with any class when you want to improve: students' commitment to acting upon feedback given; the quality of feedback given to students by their peers; students' understanding of what quality looks like by explicitly sharing the criteria of a task. Sometimes, students may underperform in a task and the teacher might be at a loss as to why this has happened; often it is due to the students' lack of clarity as to what is expected of them and/or a lack of awareness of what quality looks like for a particular piece of work. As long as you have good quality exemplars, model the feedback process to students and allow sufficient time for students to share, critique and refine their work, then this approach could have significant benefits.

Critiquing our work	
Instructions	**Criteria**
1. Sticky-tac your work up on the wall to add to our gallery.	1. A clear topic sentence **identifying** an idea about George and Lennie's friendship.
2. Sticky-tac a piece of plain paper underneath it for your peers to leave their comments related to the criteria.	2. A **quotation** that matches their topic sentence.
3. Read the work on the left and right of your piece. Leave a comment for each piece of work using the criteria on the board.	3. An **explanation** of their quotation and what it reveals about George and Lennie's friendship.
	4. Another idea from the quotation which **explores** George and Lennie's friendship.
4. After leaving your comments, go round the room and read other students' work. Pick the piece you think best fulfils the criteria for this task. Draw a star on this piece.	5. Analysing a word or phrase from the quotation focusing on what it makes the reader think or feel.
5. Return to your work, read the comments left for you and refine your piece.	6. Ending the paragraph by **evaluating** what Steinbeck wants us to think about the bigger picture, linked to the context of the novel.

Fig. 13 Example of instructions and criteria when setting up gallery critique

Academic vocabulary

Overview:

One of the best ways to raise the level of challenge in your class is to increase the demands you place on your students when communicating verbally or in writing. Being able to use academic vocabulary is a vital part of students learning how to think like an expert. It is easy for students to say the first thing that comes into their head and for the teacher to accept that response if the answer is factually accurate. Yet one of the most obvious differences between high-achieving and low-achieving students are the words that they use to articulate an idea and the confidence with which they express themselves.

Why this approach might be useful:

An effective way of challenging students is to use part of each lesson to explicitly teach academic vocabulary to your students; often the starter is an easy place to start teaching vocabulary. Decide in advance which words students will need to know that lesson and then plan how students will use these new words later, either in discussion or in a piece of writing. Students need to have vocabulary explicitly taught to them and reinforced constantly, with multiple opportunities to retrieve the vocabulary from their memory and use in the correct context; otherwise, if vocabulary is only taught once with no follow-up then the students won't remember and it will be a wasted opportunity.

Issues to consider:

In order for this approach to be effective, it's important that the teacher does not overload the students with too many new words to learn. Moreover, the teacher needs to plan carefully when they will give the students opportunities to revisit these words. Many teachers teach academic vocabulary by sharing definitions with their students but often definitions, taken out of context, aren't particularly helpful. The words need to be set in a clear context and be used in sentences in order for students to have a full understanding of their meaning.

When you might use it:

At the start of the topic, it is worth having a sheet with all of the key academic vocabulary you have planned to teach the students. Share with the students each lesson which words from the list you will be expecting them to use. Plan a range of verbal and written tasks to check that students are comfortable using the new words and are using them in the correct context.

Benefit for students:

Improved use of academic vocabulary supports students in expressing themselves articulately and coherently. When the teacher questions the students, if they don't use academic vocabulary in their responses, challenge the students to have a second attempt, reframing their response so they are completely accurate. Get the students familiar with asking themselves 'What language would a geographer/ historian/artist use?' Students can orally rehearse responses using the specified academic vocabulary before applying their knowledge in written form.

Homework

Overview:

Homework is a great way of stretching students and offering them a challenge. However, homework is often not used effectively for a number of reasons. Sometimes, teachers don't get through the lesson they've planned and so can't set the homework they've planned. At other times, it may be that the homework set is a 'more of the same' approach, consolidating the learning. Another issue can be that teachers may work in schools where they have to adhere to a homework

Key Learning Question: How does Steinbeck present the ranch as a microcosm of 1930s America?	
Academic vocabulary	**What does it mean?**
Narrative	Story
Foreshadowing	Leaving a clue
Symbolism	Signs that represent ideas
Microcosm	Small-scale version
What is the difference between narrative and plot? If you read the novel a second time, why would you be able to identify foreshadowing more easily? Can any object in the novel be an example of symbolism? Which aspects of 1930s America are highlighted through the ranch being a microcosm?	

Fig. 14 Example of challenging students to use academic vocabulary

timetable and end up setting homework when it's not the right point in the learning sequence. An effective homework task is one that either builds on the learning from the lesson or sets up the learning to come (this is also referred to as flipped learning) and gives students the opportunity to apply their knowledge independently.

Why this approach might be useful:

This approach might be useful if you have a lot of content to cover but want to give students the opportunity to work on tasks independently. Homework tasks can be stretched out over a longer period of time to allow students to really get to grips with the learning challenge set for them. You may want to offer choice and this can easily be done by creating a bank of challenging tasks for students to tackle throughout the topic.

Issues to consider:

Students sometimes don't place great value on homework and teachers can spend ages chasing students who haven't done their homework. Another issue is trying to balance the demands of classwork and homework with regards to what the teacher can realistically give feedback on. Another issue to consider is whether all students have access to resources required to complete homework tasks, such as Internet access or a particular book in the library. If you can pre-empt as many of these issues as possible, the greater chance the students will have to be able to complete the work to a good standard.

When you might use it:

Focusing on improving the quality of homework is often a sign of a classroom which has a challenging and stimulating learning environment. If you are looking to explicitly raise the level of expectations in your class, then homework is a good place to start as you are sending out the message that learning doesn't end as soon as they leave your class. Make sure that time is built in to celebrate the achievements of those students who rise to the challenge of attempting your more challenging homework tasks.

Benefit for students:

Getting students into good homework routines where they expect to be given challenging work to do outside of the classroom certainly increases their appetite for learning. At first they might resist, but if they see that their hard work is acknowledged and celebrated, then they are more likely to want to do the work. If you are going to create a homework bank of tasks with different levels of challenge, make sure that the different levels of challenge are made clear to students so you and they can monitor their progress with these tasks. The TA could be the progress monitor for the student, talking to them about what they need to do to meet the challenge and helping them to reflect on their learning by asking them questions about their work.

Homework challenge tasks: *Of Mice and Men*		
Warm Task	**Hot Task**	**Scorching Task**
Create a word list of ten keywords for *Of Mice and Men* and explain why you chose each word.	Create a Facebook profile for the main characters.	Create a presentation on the lives of women in 1930s America.
Create a timeline of key events in America that would have affected characters in *Of Mice and Men*.	Create a job advert for working on the boss's ranch.	Write up an interview between John Steinbeck and the interviewer finding out his intentions when writing *Of Mice and Men*.
Create a crossword for another student to complete.	Draw a hierarchy ladder, rank the characters' position on the ranch and annotate with your justifications.	Research the Jim Crow laws and write how they would affect the character of Crooks.

Fig. 15 Example of a homework challenge bank

Teaching assistants

Overview:

Much has been written about the effectiveness of TAs and how much impact they have on students' learning. Some argue that they are not value for money and can often ending up babysitting certain students rather than making a significant difference to student outcomes. If this is the case, then most likely it is due to a planning issue rather than a lack of willingness on the part of the TA. TAs can only support the teacher in their efforts to challenge students to make good progress if they are given enough time to digest the content of the lesson and plan how they will support students with particular learning needs to access the lesson.

Why this approach might be useful:

Having another adult working with you and giving their input into how best to support students is incredibly beneficial. TAs can have a valuable alternative perspective as their interactions with particular students may be different to your own as they may see them in several lessons across school and also have experience of a particular special educational need. If you are struggling to pitch the learning correctly for certain students then your TA should be your first port of call.

Issues to consider:

The more information you can provide for the TA, the more helpful they will be to you. Don't expect them to just turn up to the lesson and work miracles! Decide how you want to work with your TA. Which students do you want them to work with during the lesson? What exactly do you want them to do? How will you measure the impact of their work with students? What do you need to provide for the TA so they can plan accordingly? When and how often will you meet your TA to discuss the progress of particular students? These are just some of the questions you will need to consider if you are to have a fruitful relationship with your TA.

When you might use it:

Clearly, this approach is only suitable if you have been assigned a TA. However, even if you have not been assigned one, make use of their expert knowledge of particular students. Contact them and ask them what they know about a particular student and what advice they would give you to best support the student. TAs will be pleased to be involved in these important learning conversations.

Benefit for students:

Students with particular learning needs often build incredibly strong bonds with TAs as they appreciate the support they can offer to help them access the learning. If the teacher wants to increase the level of challenge for a student who works with a TA, then the TA could be the person to introduce this challenge to the student without overwhelming them.

Topic: *Of Mice and Men* How well can (insert student) do the following? Please rank from 1–5, with 5 being 'Can do this with ease'. Follow the narrative in their head ☐ Read aloud in front of their peers ☐ Ask questions for clarification ☐ Ask questions to develop their thinking ☐ Participate in a discussion ☐ Sequence information in a text ☐ Read between the lines and infer meaning ☐ Track developments in characters ☐ Structure an extended piece of writing ☐	Based on the student's needs, what is the agreed focus for how the TA will support the student during this topic?

Fig. 16 Example of an audit to assess a student's needs used by the teacher and TA

Stretch and challenge approach	Explanation
1. Learning intentions	Sharing challenging learning intentions with students so they have a clear understanding of their learning journey and how they will progress through it.
2. Independence and resilience	Increasing students' ability to work for increasingly extended periods of time without support from the teacher.
3. Questioning and discussion	Developing students' questioning and participation in group discussion to improve the quality of their thinking.
4. Choice of task	Offering a range of tasks with different levels of challenge so all students, regardless of their starting point, can access the learning and challenge themselves further.
5. Resources	Creating a range of resources for students to use to support them in accessing a challenging task but deciding when it is most appropriate to let students use them.
6. Groupings	Identifying which students should be grouped together and for which tasks to ensure they are appropriately challenged and can contribute effectively to support each other's learning.
7. Feedback	Framing feedback so that students have to take responsibility for improving their own learning and closing their learning gaps.

Stretch and challenge approach	Explanation
8. Academic vocabulary	Increasing the language demands you place on the students by explicitly teaching them academic vocabulary that they can use verbally and in writing.
9. Homework	Creating a bank of homework challenge tasks that enable students to extend their learning outside of class time.
10. Teaching assistants	Collaborating with TAs to ensure all students can access the learning and support students to challenge themselves further.

Fig. 17 Overview of the different approaches to stretch and challenge

Chapter 3 takeaway

Teaching tip

Get some feedback

Once you have thought about the ten different approaches to stretch and challenge you could use and the ones you will begin to experiment with, get some feedback from your students and colleagues. Ask students if they have noticed a difference in the way you are planning their lessons. You could ask the whole class or you could select particular students who you are trying to challenge further. After a few weeks of trying some of the approaches, ask a colleague to come in and watch you – it's always good to have a fresh pair of eyes look at your class without bias.

Pass it on

Sharing your ideas – colleagues outside your school setting

Although it is always a good idea to share your ideas with colleagues inside your own school, it is equally interesting to seek views from colleagues who aren't in your school. Often, we can become blinkered when working in a particular environment; things become normalised and colleagues who you work with will also be used to the status quo. At times, it can be really beneficial to speak to teachers from other schools; they may not be teaching in the same context as you or know the students as well as your own school colleagues but they do have a fresh pair of eyes. Ask them what they do at their school – could it work where you teach?

Don't just stay in your own phase of education either – gain insight from those who work with younger students too. In particular, work with the transition team to see what experience the students have had before coming to you and the level of challenge they were used to. We can be guilty in secondary school of underestimating just how much year 6 students can achieve! Visit their classrooms and see for yourself what younger students are being asked to learn so that you can ensure you have pitched the level of challenge appropriately.

You might want to look farther afield and connect with colleagues from outside your local area. One way of doing this is to attend a TeachMeet. You can easily search for TeachMeets by doing a Google search or by searching Twitter. If you're feeling brave, you could present at a TeachMeet, sharing with others what you have been working on. Even if the thought of presenting fills you with dread, you can always go along to listen to other teachers sharing what they're doing in their classroom and gain inspiration to try something new.

Sharing with staff in your school

If your school has its own teaching and learning hub online, you could write a short blog about your approach to stretch and challenge. If your school doesn't have an online platform for sharing, you could always send out an email with a link to something you've read. Or perhaps you could email staff to see if they'd be interested in pairing up with you and trying out a particular approach to see if it works for other students.

Alternatively, you could share your ideas at your school's weekly briefing; many schools are trying to reorganise their meeting time to ensure there is less of a focus on admin and more of a focus on teaching and learning.

Share and tweet

Share your experiences with different approaches to stretch and challenge on Twitter using the hashtag #BloomsCPD.

CPD book club recommendation

Graham Nuthall, *The Hidden Lives of Learners*
(see Bibliography and further reading, page 273)

Bloggers' corner

David Didau has some really interesting posts on his approach to stretch and challenge; follow his blog to see how his thoughts have developed over the years. www.learningspy.co.uk.

To do list:

❏ Reflect on different approaches to stretch and challenge that you have used in the past and others you might consider using in the future

❏ Tweet your experiences of the different approaches you are trying by using the hashtag #BloomsCPD

❏ Arrange a visit to another school or a conversation with a colleague from a different school to see stretch and challenge from a different perspective

❏ Set aside time to read David Didau's blog posts on challenging students further

❏ Read *The Hidden Lives of Learners* by Graham Nuthall

4

Getting to grips with the big ideas

The concept of stretch and challenge covers a range of pedagogical approaches and many important thinkers have spent time researching which approaches have the most impact on developing our learners. Many teachers wish to engage with research and find out what they can do to try and develop their practice and, in turn, their students' knowledge and understanding of the subject they teach. However, many find it difficult to find the time to read all of the research that is out there; consequently, this chapter will explore some of the key ideas of educational thinkers which may have an impact on your practice. There are too many ideas to cover in just this chapter – it would require a whole series of books – but below are some of the thinkers that have made significant contributions to the area of stretch and challenge.

Throughout this chapter, after sharing the key ideas of each educational thinker, I suggest some takeaway ideas for you to try with your students; these are clear and accessible strategies inspired by the thinkers' research. These ideas can be trialled individually or you may want to use a combination of them to stretch your students, as will be discussed further in the next chapter (see chapter 5, page 83). For ease of cross-reference, the strategies described are numbered consecutively and summarised at the end of the chapter (pages 80–81).

Writer/researcher	Specialist area	Key publication	Website	Twitter handle
Robin Alexander	Dialogic teaching	*Towards Dialogic Teaching*	www.robinalexander.org.uk	N/A
Ron Berger	Excellence	*An Ethic of Excellence*	https://vimeo.com/38247060	@RonBergerEL
Peter C. Brown, Henry L. Roediger III and Mark A. McDaniel	Learning and memory	*Make It Stick*	makeitstick.net	N/A
Carol Dweck	Mindset	*Mindset*	www.mindsetonline.com	N/A
John Hattie and Gregory Yates	Cognitive science	*Visible Learning and the Science of How We Learn*	visible-learning.org	@VisibleLearning
Doug Lemov, Erica Woolway and Katie Yezzi	Teaching techniques and practice	*Teach Like a Champion; Practice Perfect*	teachlikeachampion.com	@Doug_Lemov @EricaWoolway @ktyezzi
Robert J. Marzano and Debra J. Pickering	Academic vocabulary	*Building Academic Vocabulary*	marzanoresearch.com	@robertjmarzano
Graham Nuthall	Classroom observation and learning	*The Hidden Lives of Learners*		N/A
Gordon Stobart	Expertise	*The Expert Learner*	vimeo.com/search?q=gordon+stobart	N/A
Dylan Wiliam	Assessment for Learning	*Embedded Formative Assessment; Inside the Black Box*	dylanwiliam.org	@dylanwiliam
Daniel T. Willingham	Cognitive science	*Why Don't Students Like School?*	www.danielwillingham.com	@DTWillingham

Fig. 18 Stretch and challenge – the big ideas

Robin Alexander on Dialogic teaching

Name: Robin Alexander
Website: www.robinalexander.org.uk
What to read: *Towards Dialogic Teaching* by Robin Alexander

'... dialogue requires an interactive loop or spiral rather than linearity ... It is what happens to the answer that makes it worth uttering, and transforms it from a correct or incorrect response to a cognitive stepping stone.'

(Alexander, 2008a, p. 111)

The principle behind dialogic teaching is to develop students who can use the power of talk to stimulate and extend their thinking; by doing so, this will accelerate their learning and understanding. Using talk for cognitive rather than solely social reasons, helps us to diagnose our students' needs and assess their progress. Dialogic teaching rejects the traditional model of classroom talk that centres around the IRF model (initiate a question, listen to a student's response, give feedback on whether the response is right or wrong). The IRF model gives all the power to the teacher who poses all of the questions. Dialogic talk requires the following types of quality talk:

- interactions which encourage students to think, and to think in different ways
- questions which invite much more than simple recall
- answers which are justified, followed up and built upon
- feedback which informs and leads thinking forward
- contributions which are extended rather than simple one-word responses
- exchanges which chain together into coherent and deepening lines of enquiry
- discussion which probes and challenges rather than unquestioningly accepts.

It takes a considerable amount of time to train students to become familiar with using talk for such cognitive purposes; however, once students become confident then the cognitive challenge is greatly enhanced compared to more traditional talk in the classroom.

Putting it into practice

Below are some dialogic teaching strategies that you can try out with your classes. See what you think and adapt them where necessary depending on your own context.

Strategy 1: Philosophy for Children (P4C)

P4C begins with a stimulus that provokes thought; it could be a video clip, a photograph or a statement. Give your students some silent thinking time to get to grips with the stimulus before sharing their thoughts with their peers. The students put forward different questions they would like to discuss and debate. Once the group has decided on the discussion question, the teacher moves away from being the expert and facilitates discussion rather than leading it. The students participate in the discussion and build on each others' contributions. Whether they agree or disagree with others, the rule is to justify opinions with reasons. The end of the session involves students sharing how their opinions may have changed as a result of the dialogue.

Strategy 2: Socratic discussion

This is another specific model to introduce structured talk to students, which focuses on increasing the quality of students' thinking. The process for Socratic discussion is to ask the questions for different reasons. The different types of questions are:

- for clarification
- to probe assumptions
- to probe the evidence
- about different perspectives
- to probe implications
- about the significance of the original question.

Strategy 3: Devil's advocate

Force students to think differently by getting students, in pairs, to argue a specific viewpoint for 60 seconds, even if it is a view that they do not hold. Display a statement on the board and give the students prompt cards of things to consider in order to help them formulate an argument or viewpoint. This task is a great example of Alexander's idea about providing a cognitive stepping stone rather than just identifying correct or incorrect answers and shutting down the dialogue.

Ron Berger on Excellence

Name: Ron Berger

Twitter handle: @RonBergerEL

What to read: An Ethic of Excellence by Ron Berger

What to watch: 'Austin's Butterfly: Building Excellence in Student Work' (https://vimeo.com/38247060)

'Once a student sees that he or she is capable of excellence, that student is never quite the same. There is a new self-image, a new notion of possibility. There is an appetite for excellence.'

(Ron Berger, 2003, p. 8)

Ron Berger's book, *An Ethic of Excellence*, completely changed the way I planned for my students to produce important pieces of work. In the book, he argues that the most effective classrooms are those in which a culture of excellence has been created where students are able to critique their own work and the work of their peers confidently and knowledgeably. He believes that teachers need to have high expectations of what they think their students are capable of producing and to share their aspirational goals with their students at all times. Excellent students are those who are able to master their craft and understand that any first attempt at a piece of work is a draft, something which will need to have time and effort invested in it if it is to become a truly excellent piece of work.

He states that there are five principles that create a culture of excellence:

1. Teachers need to set work that really matters and explain to the students why the work is so important.
2. Students need to see examples of excellence so they are clear on what they are aiming for in their own work.
3. A piece of work will need several redrafts based on feedback.
4. Feedback from peers in the classroom needs to be kind, specific and helpful.
5. Students rise to the challenge of sharing their work with a real audience. Publicly presenting their work shows the students how much importance is placed on what they have produced.

Putting it into practice

Below are some strategies that you can try out with your classes. See what you think and adapt them where necessary depending on your own context.

Strategy 4: Examples of excellence

When setting tasks for your students, help them understand what is expected of them by sharing with them examples of previous students' work that has the hallmarks of excellence. Discuss with the students what makes the work excellent. If you can share a couple of examples with students, then this will help students to discuss the different aspects of the work and judge which work best meets the success criteria.

Strategy 5: Redrafting process

We are always concerned about how we are going to cover all of the curriculum content we need to but if a piece of work is going to receive substantial feedback, then consider giving students the opportunity to redraft their work based on your feedback before they hand in their finished piece. Even work that meets all of the criteria can be refined if given helpful feedback. Encourage students to hand in the first and final draft of their work to make visible how they have improved their work based on feedback. You may even want your students to annotate their work to say exactly what they have focused on to make their work better.

Strategy 6: Peer critique

Many of us are all too familiar with the pitfalls of peer assessment. Students' attempts at assessing each other's work can lack quality and comments can remain superficial and unhelpful. Pair up your students so everyone is given a feedback buddy. The role of the feedback buddy is to make three comments on their peer's work:

1. an acknowledgement of where they met the criteria
2. a specific target for improvement based on where they have not met the criteria
3. a helpful comment about how they might go about meeting their target.

Strategy 7: Public presentation

An excellent way of challenging your students is to show them that their work is valued and to find as many ways to celebrate their achievements as possible. It can be hard to get students to take an interest in their work if they think that nobody cares about what they are producing. Up the ante by telling them that the head of department is going to select their favourite pieces. Alternatively, tell them that the pieces that show the most progress from the last piece of work will be mailed home. Another way of celebrating their work is to set up market stalls where students explain what they have been working on to another class who come to visit the stalls.

Peter C. Brown, Henry L. Roediger III and Mark A. McDaniel on Learning and memory

Name: Peter C. Brown, Henry L. Roediger and Mark A. McDaniel

Website: makeitstick.net

What to read: *Make It Stick* by Peter C. Brown, Henry L. Roediger III and Mark A. McDaniel

---

'When you space out practice at a task and get a little rusty between sessions, or you interleave the practice of two or more subjects, retrieval is harder and feels less productive, but the effort produces longer lasting learning.

(Brown et al., 2014, p. 4)

Make It Stick is an excellent book that helps teachers to understand what strategies to use in order to ensure that students remember and understand difficult new concepts. It is an age-old problem we have all faced: why can't my students remember what I taught them last term when I spent ages planning that scheme of work?!

One problem is the way that many schools design their curriculum with chunked units of work. This can also be applied to revision time. Instead of chunking the curriculum – traditionally half-termly units of work with an end of topic test before moving onto the next unit – the authors suggest interleaving. Interleaving is the process of introducing a new concept or topic, then layering in a new concept or topic and then returning to the original concept or topic. This process is repeated several times depending on curriculum time. The authors argue that the most powerful way for students to remember what you've taught them is to force them to retrieve information just when they're on the brink of forgetting the information. This is called 'effortful retrieval' and making the brain work hard to remember helps the students' long-term memories.

Another issue the authors cover is that students are very good at thinking they know something when, in fact, they don't really know it all. They've tricked themselves into thinking they know something because they are using passive revision strategies such as re-reading familiar notes or highlighting bits of texts; better options are ones which force the students to think metacognitively about their learning and to test themselves.

Finally, the authors state that all learning requires a strong foundation of knowledge, so it is important that teachers support students in building a strong foundation of prior knowledge to help them make connections between different pieces of new information. Mastering key concepts and going over them many times is important before moving on too quickly to something new.

Putting it into practice

Below are some strategies that you can try out with your classes. See what you think and adapt them where necessary depending on your own context.

Strategy 8: Desirable difficulties

To ensure that students really have understood what you have taught them, introduce desirable difficulties – such as a new piece of conflicting information or a withdrawal of a scaffold – to see how students react to this change. If they have understood what you have taught them, then they should be able to adapt and respond in light of the desirable difficulty.

Strategy 9: Frequent, low-stakes quizzes

Many students hate the idea of tests but that is often because they are seen as high-stakes and competitive. The idea of low-stakes, frequent quizzing is different; it is part of a routine that supports students and teachers in understanding how much has been learnt. Get the students into a routine of knowing that there will be a weekly or fortnightly quiz and that the content in it will be not just present material but material from previous learning. Students can co-construct the quizzes with different students taking responsibility for planning some of the questions.

Strategy 10: Generative learning

It seems odd, but the authors state that getting students to solve a problem before being taught any of the new concepts or methods actually leads to better results, as noted in several studies mentioned by the authors. However, this is not a new idea, as the authors state: 'Generation is another name for old-fashioned trial and error.' (Brown et al., 2014, p.94) The idea behind generative learning is that learning is stronger when students invest more effort in trying to find a solution than if they passively sit back and let the teacher talk at them. When the students do encounter new information, they already have some sort of framework based on them trying to work something out earlier. For example, if you practise a maths equation before being told the steps to take to work out the question, you will do better once you are given the information as the brain has had to put in effort to try and work it out.

Carol Dweck on Mindset

Name: Carol Dweck
Website: www.mindsetonline.com
What to read: *Mindset* by Carol Dweck
What to watch: 'Developing a Growth Mindset' (www.youtube.com/watch?v=hiiEeMN7vbQ)

'. . . people with the growth mindset thrive when they're stretching themselves. When do people with the fixed mindset thrive? When things are safely within their grasp. If things get too challenging – when they're not feeling smart or talented – they lose interest.'

(Dweck, 2012, p. 17)

Carol Dweck's work focuses on the different characteristics of learners. Learners either have a fixed or growth mindset. There are five areas to consider when working out what type of mindset a student has in your class:

1. challenges
2. obstacles
3. effort
4. criticism
5. success of others.

Some students can have a fixed mindset which means that they believe intelligence is fixed. These students are interested in wanting to look smart and avoid failure. They give up easily because they don't recognise the link between effort and achievement, ignoring negative feedback. They feel threatened by the success of other students in their class.

On the other hand, students with a growth mindset believe that their intelligence can be developed. These students are interested in learning and embrace challenges. They keep persevering even when they experience failure because they believe that the harder they try, the more likely it is they will get better. In order to improve, they encourage constructive criticism as they see its value in helping them master new knowledge and skills. They seek out stories of inspirational figures and try and see what they can learn from their stories.

Interestingly, students with varied school experience can fall into the fixed mindset category. We have all taught very high-achieving students for whom lots of things seem to come easily to them; however, when they come up against something that is challenging, they don't know what to do and give up, often blaming others for their failure. Similarly, we've all taught students who have had rather negative experiences at schools and state openly that they are no good at certain subjects so there's no point in trying. The goal for us as teachers is to identify which of our students have a fixed mindset and to work with them to see the link between effort and achievement.

Putting it into practice

Below are some strategies that you can try out with your classes. See what you think and adapt them where necessary depending on your own context.

Strategy 11: Student learning audit

Create an audit of the learning skills you would like your students to have. Ask students to complete this audit of their skills and then schedule one-to-one time with those students who you feel need to develop particular skills. Talk with them about how they could show themselves and you how they are actively trying to develop particular skills in the next unit of work. During the unit, students can refer back to their audit and see where they are making improvements.

Strategy 12: Ownership of feedback

When your students are given feedback from either yourself or from peers, how do your students react? Do they acknowledge the feedback and actively go about closing their learning gaps or do they ignore the feedback they've been given? Set aside time after students receive feedback to hold them to account about how they are going to make improvements. Make each student write down what action they are going to take and negotiate with you what they will show you as evidence of them taking action. It could be that they make a short instructional video, redo the test or create a set of flashcards to learn from.

Strategy 13: Reinforce growth mindset through homework

Get your students to identify something they have struggled with in the past. Their homework could be to return to that topic and commit to revising it so that they can create a revision resource for another member of the class. This will give the student a sense of achievement so that they will go from believing themselves to be rubbish at something to becoming an expert in a particular area. Having to create something for a peer increases the student's sense of accountability for improving their knowledge.

John Hattie and Gregory Yates on Cognitive science

Name: John Hattie and Gregory Yates
Website: visible-learning.org
What to read: *Visible Learning and the Science of How We Learn* by John Hattie and Gregory Yates

---

'... it helps when students want to learn, want to be challenged ... This invokes the Goldilocks principle of not making the challenge or success too hard or too easy relative to where the student currently is.'

(Hattie et al., 2014, p. xiii)

John Hattie is well known amongst teachers for his previous books, *Visible Learning* and the follow-up *Visible Learning for Teachers*, and the book featured here, *Visible Learning and the Science of How We Learn*, which takes our understanding one step further by focusing on how students' brains work based on extensive global research.

Hattie and Yates argue that most of us as learners need a trusting, fair and safe environment to acknowledge that 'we do not know' and will make errors in learning. The first step to challenging students is to make your students comfortable enough to say when they do not know something rather than trying to hide it. Use this moment as a way to challenge them; students need to realise that persistence, concentration and deliberate practice are the keys to success. Deliberate practice is a goal-directed activity. Students are presented with tasks that are initially outside of their current performance level but the tasks can be mastered by focusing on critical aspects and refining technique through repetition and feedback.

Linked to this, help-seeking is more likely to be seen in students who have strong levels of intrinsic motivation. This intrinsic motivation is often referred to as 'mastery goal orientation' when students want to learn new knowledge because they believe they will acquire better understanding. This type of learning is contrasted with performance orientation which focuses more on looking good and outperforming others in the class. The key, then, is to encourage all students in your class to view help-seeking as a sign of effective learning rather than protecting their egos.

Another part of the book focuses on how teachers as activators rather than facilitators have a much stronger average effect size (0.61 compared to 0.19). When the teacher is an activator of learning, they:

- teach students to self-verbalise
- develop their own teacher clarity, including explanations, modelling and scaffolding learning
- set up reciprocal teaching
- give clear and useful feedback
- teach metacognitive strategies
- use direct instruction
- set up learning sequences with the goal of mastery learning
- provide worked examples.

Putting it into practice

Below are some strategies that you can try out with your classes. See what you think and adapt them where necessary depending on your own context.

Strategy 14: Find and fix errors

Students need to get used to seeing error as completely normal and a good opportunity to learn from. Create a culture in the class in which students are used to having their work shared with their peers and used as a discussion stimulus. You would highlight errors in the work but not state explicitly to your students why they are errors; it is their job to find out why they are errors. This task can be easily made more challenging by not highlighting all of the errors and making students find the remaining errors in the piece of work.

Strategy 15: Help desk

To encourage your students to become help-seeking rather than too dependent on you or a particular resource, set up a help desk in your classroom with a range of resources that might be useful to students. Before starting a task, get your students to discuss what they will need to do to be successful and what they might find difficult. Set all students off without any help and then create windows of time when students can visit the help desk if they feel they need extra support. Once they have finished their piece of work, get the students to write a commentary about what help they made use of so they get into the habit of being responsible for their own learning.

Strategy 16: Deliberate practice RAG checklist

In advance of an important assessment, create a checklist which breaks down all of the knowledge and skills required to produce an excellent piece of work. Get students to go through the checklist and RAG (red, amber, green) their knowledge and skill level: red for unconfident, amber for OK but need to do more practice on this and green for very confident. Use this information to set up some deliberate practice sessions where students hone their skills before the assessment. To make it easier for you and peers to give feedback, seat students with other students who are working on the same knowledge or skill.

Doug Lemov on Teaching techniques and practice

Name: Doug Lemov

Twitter handle: @Doug_Lemov

Website: teachlikeachampion.com

What to read: *Teach Like a Champion* by Doug Lemov, *Practice Perfect* by Doug Lemov, Erica Woolway and Katie Yezzi

What to watch: 'Doug Lemov on Teach Like a Champion' (www.youtube.com/watch?v=1XpWbDjhIiI)

'In practice you can master a skill thoroughly or not at all … Either way, what you do is likely to become encoded – it will be instilled in muscle memory or mental circuitry and become habit – for better or worse.'

(Lemov et al., 2012, p. 25)

Doug Lemov has revolutionised American schools with his book *Teach Like a Champion* and the book he co-authored: *Practice Perfect*. What makes these books so useful is there are clear techniques and rules to implement in your classroom. The techniques chosen in both books are based on countless observations of highly-effective classroom teachers. He poses the question: 'What makes these teachers so effective and what can we learn from them?'

In *Teach Like a Champion*, there are several techniques that focus on raising your expectations of what students say and do in your classroom. Three techniques in particular are helpful in challenging our students to improve their learning: 'right is right'; 'stretch it'; 'break it down'.

'Right is right' makes explicit to students if their answer is indeed right. This may seem pretty obvious but how many times do we as teachers say, 'Yes, good', to an answer that isn't actually 100 percent correct? Often we do this because we don't want to show a student up or put them off from answering more questions; sometimes we're so thankful that certain students are even participating that we'll say anything to keep them interested! The problem with this is that it's actually an example of low expectations in disguise. We're not doing our students any favours if we're accepting answers that aren't 100 percent correct. If we wouldn't accept the answer from the highest-achieving student in the class, then we shouldn't accept it from any other student.

'Stretch it' focuses on looking for any opportunity to extend the thinking of your students. It doesn't require pre-planned resources as it's a technique that is responsive to students' answers. This technique encourages students to develop their initial correct answer by adding another dimension to their response. The message we're sending out to our students is that learning never stops – just because you've given an answer doesn't mean you're off the hook.

'Break it down' supports students in attempting tasks that initially may seem too challenging; a task which might normally elicit a response from a student of, 'I can't do it. It's too hard'. This technique offers a range of ideas about how to get started; Lemov believes that most students, once they've made a start, will want to carry on trying but often don't know where to start with a daunting task or question.

Moving on to *Practice Perfect*, this book focuses on techniques that enable teachers to get students to practise in a more effective way. This book is particularly useful for thinking about how you would set up learning for a major assessment. Once you decide what it is you are expecting the student to do, how are you going to help them practise the skills they need to excel?

Six ideas about practice are important when we consider how we can challenge students to improve their performance:

1. Practice makes permanent so be careful not to try and practise too many things at once as it will slow down learning.

2. Teach skills in a sequence of objectives where each skill is increasingly more challenging.
3. After practising a skill, correct rather than critique to close the learning gap immediately.
4. Devise opportunities for practice that support students to know which skill to use in the right situation.
5. Model a skill to students but also verbally describe your thought process to give students a better chance of practising correctly.
6. Be explicit with students about what you are modelling and why it is an important skill.

Putting it into practice

Below are some strategies that you can try out with your classes. See what you think and adapt them where necessary depending on your own context.

Strategy 17: Right is right – oral rehearsal

To increase the quality of students' responses, give them some time to work out how they will respond to your question and practise by having an oral rehearsal. Randomly select a handful of students to stand up and verbalise their response. The class decides which answer or answers are 100 percent correct and comments on the content and the vocabulary used. The teacher's role is to draw out some of the subtleties in the students' responses rather than to say straight away which answers are best.

Strategy 18: Stretch it – upgrade initial responses

This can be done as a whole class, using a random generator to decide how to upgrade the response or it can be done in pairs, with the students going through all of the following steps. When students answer a question correctly, they could be asked to: explain how or why they know their answer is correct, replace some of their word choices with more sophisticated vocabulary, provide specific evidence from the stimulus text, apply their answer in a different context.

Strategy 19: Break it down – prompt for success

When you set up a challenging task, offer a thinking prompt to get your students off to a positive start. Ask them to provide: an example they know, a context to the task, a rule they need to know to tackle the task, the first step they could take to get started, false choices they could eliminate or narrow down their options. These prompts could easily be made into a laminated resource card that students get familiar using or students could work in pairs to question each other using these prompts before settling down to work independently.

Strategy 20: A set of task instructions

If a task requires students to work on it for an extended period of time, then one way you can support students is to provide a clear set of instructions for success. If students are more confident, they can always write their own set of instructions that they can tick off as they go along. Encourage students to write out the instructions in small steps using imperatives.

Strategy 21: Shorten the feedback loop

You can't always give students immediate feedback which is why it is so important to train students to be effective feedback buddies. It is not always necessary to set up a critique; sometimes, identifying errors and correcting them is more beneficial. Display a list of possible errors on the board and get students to look at each other's work and see if they can find any of these errors.

Strategy 22: Model and describe

Invite a student to come to the front of the class and model a skill for the rest of the class. Ask them to verbalise what they are doing and why they are doing it. Get the student to pause and invite questions and responses from the rest of the class. Are they doing it correctly? Is there a better way?

Robert Marzano and Debra Pickering on Academic vocabulary

Name: Robert Marzano and Debra Pickering

Twitter handle: @robertjmarzano

Website: www.marzanoresearch.com

What to read: *Building Academic Vocabulary* by Robert Marzano and Debra Pickering

What to watch: 'Building Basic Vocabulary with Dr. Robert J. Marzano' (www.youtube.com/watch?v=L_HNo9Wos4o)

'Vocabulary development and knowledge are crucial for students' success. Vocabulary is a fundamental aspect of reading and literacy, and it also allows students to think about information and experiences in broader and deeper ways.'

(Marzano et al., 2013, *Vocabulary for the Common Core*, p. 51)

Robert Marzano and Debra Pickering highlight in their book, Building Academic Vocabulary, the link between student success and vocabulary knowledge. Most students have no problem with tier 1 words; these are everyday words that we see all the time. However, if students have a vast vocabulary base, not only will they be able to articulate their thoughts coherently and cogently (tier 2 academic words), they will also be able to build layers of knowledge by making connections between words (tier 3 technical words).

Most students are told to look up words in a dictionary to find out their definition but the authors state this has little impact on building a student's vocabulary as we learn words in context. There are six steps to effective vocabulary instruction which we can use with our students to challenge them to think and speak like an expert:

1. Provide a description, explanation, or example of the new word.
2. Ask students to create their own description, explanation, or example in their own words.
3. Ask students to construct a picture, pictograph, or symbolic representation of the word.
4. Engage students in activities that help them add to their knowledge of the words in their vocabulary notebooks.
5. Ask students regularly to discuss the words with their peers so the words' meanings are not forgotten.
6. Involve students in games that enable them to play with the words they have learnt.

Putting it into practice

Below are some strategies that you can try out with your classes. See what you think and adapt them where necessary depending on your own context.

Strategy 23: Vocabulary notebooks

Give each student a notebook in which they can track their progress in how their vocabulary is expanding. Set up the notebook so there is a page for each word. Divide the page into: the word, an example, a sentence using the word, a visual representation, synonyms and antonyms.

Strategy 24: Vocabulary upgrade

Give students a passage of text with easy words highlighted. Ask students to replace these words with more academic (tier 2) choices or technical (tier 3) choices. Students share their new versions of the text with their peers. You can then select a few examples and use them as a stimulus for whole-class discussion.

Strategy 25: Vocabulary games revision

To revise key words, ask students to create a vocabulary game which will be used as the starters or plenaries for a series of lessons. To ensure that the games they make are of good quality, provide the students with a sheet of example games to get them started. Good vocabulary games include bingo, Jeopardy™, Taboo™, odd one out and Pictionary™.

Graham Nuthall on Classroom observation and learning

Name: Graham Nuthall

What to read: *The Hidden Lives of Learners* by Graham Nuthall

'Students need several ... different interactions with relevant content for that content to be processed in their working memory and integrated into their long-term memory in such a way that it becomes part of their knowledge and beliefs.'

(Nuthall, 2007, p. 103)

Graham Nuthall's seminal work, *The Hidden Lives of Learners*, explores how children really do learn in the classroom. Based on countless observations of children, Nuthall considers the different factors that come into play when working out whether students have really learnt something or if they are just superficially performing in that particular moment. After observing groups of students for several months, he would return to the same group months later to see what their memory was of what they had learnt. Based on students' responses, Nuthall worked out what teachers could do to increase the likelihood of students remembering what they have been taught.

One key idea is to design learning activities with students' memories in mind because students need to revisit concepts on at least three different occasions if the learning is to go into a student's long-term memory. This is clearly an important idea when we are often rushing to get through curriculum content but it is imperative we plan for opportunities for students to experience that new piece of learning multiple times.

Secondly, Nuthall states that teachers often have no idea how much their students have learnt because of the input of the teacher or whether they knew it already; many teachers do not take the time to find out what the students know already and then plan accordingly to accelerate their learning. Students with good prior knowledge who have been exposed to stimulating learning opportunities will tend to do well in tests but actually they may have learnt very little as the teacher taught knowledge and skills they already had.

Thirdly, the peer culture is absolutely critical as it has considerable influence – positive or negative – on how students learn. In fact, Nuthall says that most of what students learn comes from their peers so it is essential that we spend time setting up a positive learning environment for peers to support each other rather than hinder the learning process.

Finally, teachers should encourage students to manage their own learning activities and support them in developing their metacognitive skills, as those students who were able to reflect accurately on what they could and couldn't do during a topic had greater success with their learning and were able to move out of the superficial performance zone and move onto deep learning.

Putting it into practice

Below are some strategies that you can try out with your classes. See what you think and adapt them where necessary depending on your own context.

Strategy 26: Mind maps

Before beginning a new topic, get students to create a mind map of what they already know. Using this information, test the students so you have accurate baseline data on what they know already; this will help you to plan activities that will truly stretch your students and accelerate their learning. As the unit progresses, encourage students to add to their mind map.

Strategy 27: Revisit threshold concepts

Using Nuthall's formula that students need to encounter a new idea in full at least three times for it to be stored into their long-term memory, create opportunities for students to revisit ideas throughout the topic. Decide in advance what the threshold concepts are for the topic the students are studying and encourage them to reflect on what they understand about these threshold concepts at different points using learning logs or their mind maps.

Strategy 28: Group accountability

If peers account for 80 percent of the information that students interact with in class, then we need to make sure that what students are saying to each other is useful and accurate. When setting up pair or group activities, make sure each student is held to account by assigning them a specific role or responsibility so that each student has to feed into the larger task with the specific learning they have been given to do. Ensure you monitor each group's output in case there are misconceptions that need to be cleared up quickly before moving onto something new.

Gordon Stobart on Expertise

Name: Gordon Stobart
What to read: *The Expert Learner* by Gordon Stobart
What to watch: vimeo.com/search?q=gordon+stobart

'Experts put themselves through often gruelling practice schedules, though paradoxically they see this deliberate practice as a source of engagement and pleasure. Their development has often been encouraged by multipliers that bring success and further opportunities.'

(Stobart, 2014, pp. 162-163)

Stobart researched what makes certain people experts in their different fields and disciplines. He highlights that there is still the myth of natural talent but argues that there are actually several aspects that experts share which aren't as glamorous as the 'talent' myth. Stobart shares the following information about how experts learn.

Experts learn by:

- studying the grandmasters
- seeing and understanding the bigger picture
- having opportunities and the motivation to succeed
- committing to extensive and long-term deliberate practice
- organising their extensive knowledge by making connections so it can be readily accessed
- reflecting on thought processes and methods as well as content.

By studying the craft of those experts that have gone before, learners are inspired by them and want to emulate their success. Learners also understand how all the pieces of the learning puzzle fit together, making connections between new knowledge and skills they learn. Teachers need to create as many opportunities for learners to practise and develop their understanding as they can, but this practice won't count for much unless it is well-structured and deliberate; learners need intrinsic motivation rather than external rewards to embrace new ideas and concepts. Finally, learners need to organise all of their knowledge in such a way that allows them to draw upon it when needed; expert learners tend to see the processes and methods behind the learning, making it easier to form connections and build their knowledge base.

Putting it into practice

Below are some strategies that you can try out with your classes. See what you think and adapt them where necessary depending on your own context.

Strategy 29: Find and share excellence

Encourage students to research an expert in their field for homework. What made them great? What can they learn from their work? Once they have identified what made their work excellent, they can try and emulate them. This also works when looking at previous students' work as it encourages students to aim for excellence once they know exactly what it looks like.

Strategy 30: Learning wall

To support students in understanding how all the different pieces of learning fit together into a bigger picture, create a whole-class learning wall display or have a template for each student. Throughout the topic, students can add 'bricks' to their wall, making connections between the various learning objectives.

Strategy 31: Set and reflect on targets

Students can use the feedback they receive from you or their peers to decide on their own plan of action to improve their understanding of a particular topic. Students decide on a range of homework tasks they will complete which will support them in meeting the targets they have set for themselves. After they have completed their tasks, encourage students to reflect on how they know they have developed their understanding from the start of the topic.

Dylan Wiliam on Assessment for Learning

Name: Dylan Wiliam

Twitter handle: @dylanwiliam

website: dylanwiliam.org

What to read: *Embedded Formative Assessment* by Dylan Wiliam, *Inside The Black Box* by Paul Black and Dylan Wiliam

What to watch: 'Embedded Formative Assessment' (www.youtube.com/watch?v=B3HRvFsZHoo)

'... when formative assessment practices are integrated into the minute-to-minute and day-to-day ... activities of teachers, substantial increases in student achievement ... are possible, even when outcomes are measured with externally mandated standardized tests.'

(Wiliam, 2011, pp. 160-161)

Dylan Wiliam explores the importance of using evidence of students' learning to adapt teaching and learning to meet students' needs. He discusses five core principles of how formative assessment can challenge students to improve their learning.

The first principle is that feedback needs to move the learner forward. Unfortunately, despite assessment for learning being around for 15 years, students are still receiving feedback that isn't focused on moving the learner forward; instead, students receive grades or the comments they do receive do not focus on what the student did successfully with suggestions for specific improvement that can be implemented by the student.

Clarifying, sharing and understanding learning intentions and criteria for success are vital if students are to engage in the learning process and move forward. Just putting the learning objective up on the board and getting the students to copy it down doesn't count as engaging with the objective! Once students are clear on the 'how' and 'why' of learning, as well as the 'what' of learning, students can begin to take responsibility for creating successful pieces of work.

Linked to this, students who are absolutely clear about what they are trying to achieve will be able to reflect on their learning. Those who are able to reflect on their learning can take ownership and understand the role they have to play in improving themselves – it's not just the teacher's job to develop students' learning.

Activating students as teaching resources for one another is an important feature of assessment for learning. Classrooms where students are not only responsible for their own learning but the learning of their peers too, create a stimulating and engaging environment.

Wiliam also discusses the core principle that participation in learning needs to be viewed as compulsory: there is no opt-out. In order for all students to actively participate in the lessons, teachers need to engineer effective discussion, questioning and tasks that elicit evidence of learning. Once students feel like they are a valued participant of their class, the more likely they are to continue to work hard.

Putting it into practice

Below are some strategies that you can try out with your classes. See what you think and adapt them where necessary depending on your own context.

Strategy 32: Preflight checklists
Before students hand in a piece of work, get your students into a routine of having their 'feedback buddy' complete a preflight checklist. This checklist should work as the success criteria for the piece of work. Students are working to improve each other and take responsibility for ensuring the work is ready for submission. If there are features of the work that aren't good enough or aren't evidenced at all then there is still time to add to the work before submission.

Strategy 33: Peer support
Increase your students' independence by becoming less reliant on the teacher; one way of doing this is to activate your students as peer support for each other. Strategies that could be used with your class include 'phone a friend' or 'think, pair, share'. Another technique could be to display red or green discs depending on how confident you are in your understanding. Green disc students are responsible

for teaching red disc students until everyone in the class has mastered the new content and is ready to move on.

Strategy 34: Students design their own tests

In order to judge whether students have a full understanding of the material being studied, get them to create tests for each other. Make this a structured and useful activity by modelling good and bad questions to include in the test. Students will need to know the answers to the questions before they can administer the test for their partner so this is an effective way of enabling the student to know whether they've mastered the content.

Strategy 35: Pose big questions

To see whether students have understood a new concept beyond a superficial level, pose big questions that require them to retrieve specific knowledge, apply it to a particular context and bring in additional knowledge that links to the big question. To make it more challenging for the students, have multiple choice options for the big question where all answers could possibly be correct but only one truly captures all aspects of the big picture of learning.

Daniel Willingham on cognitive science

Name: Daniel Willingham

Twitter handle: @DTWillingham

Website: www.danielwillingham.com

What to read: *Why don't students like school?* by Daniel Willingham

What to watch: 'Brain based education: fad or breakthrough' (www.youtube.com/ watch?v=vdJ7JWoLgVs)

'Thinking occurs when you combine information (from the environment and long-term memory) in new ways. That combining happens in working memory . . . knowing how to combine and rearrange ideas in working memory is essential to successful thinking.'

(Willingham, 2009, pp. 11-12)

The eye-catching title of Daniel Willingham's book, *Why Don't Students Like School?*, has made a real breakthrough in getting teachers to engage with cognitive science and consider how it may influence their classroom practice.

One statement that Willingham makes is that the mind is not naturally well-suited for thinking; thinking is slow, effortful and has uncertain outcomes. As a result, many students don't want to think hard! Moreover, our brains rely on memory and follow paths we've taken before or have seen other people take but our memory of events isn't always accurate.

Students' levels of curiosity are enhanced when they have some prior knowledge as this makes it easier to piece ideas together; students feel more confident tackling new information if they think they know something already. Therefore, students with narrower frames of reference find it more difficult to learn than those who have a wider frame of reference about a topic.

The quality of students' thinking is influenced strongly by whatever the working memory can access immediately but the quality of thinking reduces quickly once cognitive load increases. As a result, we need to ensure that our students do not experience cognitive overload, which happens when students have lots of (seemingly) unrelated information floating around in their brains where connections haven't been highlighted and organised accordingly.

Putting it into practice

Below are some strategies that you can try out with your classes. See what you think and adapt them where necessary depending on your own context.

Strategy 36: Ask 'Why?'

Force students to think about a text they are reading rather than just passively skim over it. Break down texts into chunks and have either a set of pre-created questions challenging the students to look for particular meaning or get students to create their own 'why?' questions once they gain confidence in reading for meaning.

Strategy 37: Knowledge organisers

The knowledge organiser is a tool that supports students in remembering the key knowledge they need to know before they can move on to a new concept or topic. Be clear with students about what they need to include on the knowledge organiser; ideally it should fit onto one page of A4. Students build up a bank of knowledge organisers over time – a much better use of time than re-reading notes or highlighting chunks of text. This will require students to retrieve knowledge, and using it in a different format strengthens memory. Depending on how often you see your classes, this might be every week, fortnight or half-termly.

Strategy 38: Plan for forgetting

Use homework time to assign students previously learnt topics, and challenge them to revise the material and take short quizzes to test how much they remember. The larger the gap between teaching the content and then taking the test, the harder the brain has to work to retrieve the information.

Stretch and Challenge

Technique	Description
1. Philosophy for Children (P4C)	Using a stimulus to create questions which provoke thought and debate amongst the students.
2. Socratic discussion	Following a structured approach in pairs or small groups to interrogate a question.
3. Devil's advocate	Forcing students to acknowledge other viewpoints and create an argument for a particular viewpoint.
4. Examples of excellence	Providing examples of excellent work from previous students to set the benchmark for excellence.
5. Redrafting process	Receiving feedback on a piece of work before attempting another draft to improve the initial piece.
6. Peer critique	Pairing up students to become feedback buddies for each other to support each other in improving their work.
7. Public presentation	Finding opportunities for students to share their work with a real audience and celebrate their achievements.
8. Desirable difficulties	Introducing desirable difficulties to encourage students to adapt to new ideas or stimuli.
9. Frequent, low-stakes quizzes	Creating quizzes which include current and previous learning which check how much students have learnt.
10. Generative learning	Solving a problem before being taught any new concepts to increase students' effort in trying to find solutions.
11. Student learning audit	Auditing students' skills before beginning a new topic with the aim of developing core skills throughout that unit.
12. Ownership of feedback	Holding students to account to take an active role in evidencing that they have closed their learning gaps.
13. Reinforce growth mindset through homework	Using homework to revisit topics students have struggled with and creating resources for other students.
14. Find and fix errors	Normalising errors and using them as learning opportunities to discuss how to improve their work.
15. Help desk	Setting up a help desk for students to make use of rather than relying on the teacher giving them the resources.
16. Deliberate practice RAG checklist	Devising checklists before assessments where students are responsible for checking how much their partner knows.
17. Right is right - oral rehearsal	Providing time for students to practise their response verbally before committing their answers to paper.
18. Stretch it - upgrade initial responses	Improving initial answers from students by asking them to extend their thinking or choose better vocabulary.
19. Break it down - prompt for success	Offering a range of thinking prompts to support students who are struggling to get started and work independently.
20. A set of task instructions	Providing a set of step-by-step instructions to enable students to work independently for a longer period of time.
21. Shorten the feedback loop	Displaying a list of possible errors on the board and getting feedback buddies to identify and correct errors.
22. Model and describe	Modelling a skill but verbalising the internal thought process to make explicit how students are learning.
23. Vocabulary notebooks	Developing students' academic vocabulary by using a notebook to capture new words.
24. Vocabulary upgrade	Reading texts and highlighting particular words that can be upgraded to more sophisticated vocabulary.
25. Vocabulary games revision	Playing literacy games to support students in revisiting words they have encountered and using them in context.
26. Mind maps	Creating mind maps before beginning a new topic to show prior learning and adding new knowledge during the topic.
27. Revisit threshold concepts	Planning for students to encounter a new idea at least three times so it can be stored in their long-term memory.
28. Group accountability	Assigning specific roles or responsibilities to increase students' participation and accountability.

Technique	Description
29. Find and share excellence	Identifying experts in different fields and considering how students can try and emulate their success.
30. Learning wall	Creating a whole-class learning wall display where students add new knowledge and make connections.
31. Set and reflect on targets	Setting targets based on previous feedback and students setting themselves homework to close their learning gaps.
32. Preflight checklists	Creating a checklist that students use to highlight areas that need improving before doing or submitting their work.
33. Peer support	Setting up opportunities for peers to support each other first before going to the teacher for help.
34. Students design their own tests	Designing tests for peers to complete with the aim of students checking how much they know when creating the test.
35. Pose big questions	Posing a question which forces students to apply their knowledge to a particular context and make connections.
36. Ask 'Why?'	Breaking down texts into chunks and having a series of questions for students to use to interrogate the text.
37. Knowledge organisers	Creating knowledge organisers to repackage the information they have been taught in a new format.
38. Plan for forgetting	Using homework time to assign previously learnt topics and create quizzes to test how much they remember.

Fig. 19 Summary: stretch and challenge strategies that work

Chapter 4 takeaway

Teaching tip

Keep track of your students' progress

Sometimes it's difficult to keep track of all the things your students are learning. Tracking students' progress is really important but not to be confused with writing their grades in your mark book. Make a note of particular skills and knowledge students have evidenced throughout the topic and share this information with your students. Creating an assessment matrix which focuses on actual content and skills rather than scores or grades, makes the data more meaningful and will allow you to have useful conversations with your students about what they can do to improve.

Pass it on

Sharing your ideas – get blogging

There are a number of free, easy to use platforms you could set up to start a blog. Many teachers use WordPress to write about their classroom experiences and share them with other teachers. It is easy to share a link to your blog via Twitter every time you write something new. If you are not quite ready to set up a blog, you could always contribute to staffrm. io, an online forum for sharing short blogs of 500 words on any topic that interests you. It's an excellent way of widening our contexts and seeing things from the different perspectives of those involved in education.

Students on board

Make your students part of the process once you have decided which strategies you want to try out. Share with them new approaches you are taking and ask them whether they think they are helpful or not. Explain to them exactly what it is you are trying to achieve but also be honest with them that some of the new strategies might not work out. If you can explain the research behind the strategies, then this may encourage reluctant students to become more open to new ways of being taught.

Share and tweet

Share your experiences with these new strategies and which ones already work for you on Twitter using the hashtag #BloomsCPD.

CPD book club recommendation

Zoë Elder, *Full On Learning*
(see Bibliography and further reading, page 272)

Bloggers' corner

Joe Kirby has some interesting posts on curriculum design and building strong foundations of knowledge. Visit his blog at https://pragmaticreform.wordpress.com.

TO DO LIST:

- ❏ Try out some of the strategies discussed in this chapter and see which ones have a positive impact on your students
- ❏ Share with the students what you are trying to achieve and get feedback from them about what is working well
- ❏ Decide which of the educational thinkers you want to engage with on a deeper level and start reading their books or listening to their presentations
- ❏ Get on Twitter and start following the educationalists recommended in this chapter
- ❏ Tweet your thoughts on the ideas discussed in this chapter and your experiences of using the strategies using the hashtag #BloomsCPD
- ❏ Check out Joe Kirby's blog at https://pragmaticreform.wordpress.com/
- ❏ Read *Full On Learning* by Zoë Elder

5 Putting it into practice

Having looked at the different approaches to stretch and challenge in chapter 3 (page 33) and then explored a range of strategies for challenging students in chapter 4 (page 57), the purpose of this chapter is to begin to think about how to put these into practice for your students and classes.

There are myriad strategies you could try but you need to be careful not to try and change too much too soon as this can be overwhelming for students. Instead, consider a few strategies you could implement and give students time to adjust to the new ways of working. Sometimes we are guilty of trying new approaches and then giving up on them after just a few lessons; any changes you make to your practice will need at least a term to really see if they are having a positive impact on the students' learning. As always, before trying anything new you need to look at the available information you have on the student(s) to identify what their barriers for learning are so you can work out the best way to remove them. Below, I outline the cycle I use to establish which strategies to implement for particular students with the aim of stretching them further.

This chapter presents a range of scenarios that teachers encounter in their lessons. Some scenarios are focused on individual students, groups of students or whole class. These scenarios are based on teachers I have worked with who have agreed to trial the strategies from the previous chapter. Look at the scenarios and consider which ones are similar to the students and classes you are teaching.

Stretch and challenge cycle

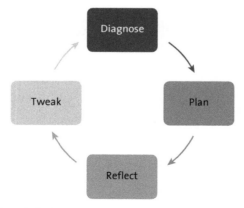

Fig. 20 The stretch and challenge cycle

Removing barriers for learning to develop students' learning

This cycle is one approach to trialling new strategies and evaluating what impact they have had on your students. This is by no means the only approach to increasing the level of challenge students experience, but I prefer this cycle as it allows time for teachers to diagnose barriers for learning, plan strategies to remove them, reflect on the impact of these strategies and further tweak their practice to continue stretching their students.

Diagnose: what are the students' barriers for learning?

This first stage in the cycle is crucial as you need to be really clear about the possible reasons as to why your students may not be accelerating with their learning. They may have several barriers that impact on their learning and you will need to identify, using a range of data available, which barriers are causing the greatest issue to the students. Without clear diagnosis, your planned stretch and challenge approach may not have the success you had hoped for.

- How does the student participate in lessons?
- What do they feel comfortable doing in lessons?
- What do they feel less comfortable doing in lessons?
- What does their latest progress data from assessments tell you about the progress they are making?
- What is their attitude to learning?
- What other information do you know about the students that would impact on their progress?

Plan: which strategies will be implemented?

Once you have diagnosed students' barriers for learning, you will need to consider the options available. There could be several strategies to try out or a just one particular approach that could make all the difference in overcoming these barriers. Remember not to overload the students with too many changes all at once, otherwise the changes to practice could be overwhelming.

- What do you hope will be achieved by implementing these particular strategies?
- How will you implement these strategies in the specific context of your classes and students?
- Are the strategies aimed at one student, a group of students or a whole class?
- Why do you think these particular strategies will have the best impact on stretching students with their learning?

Reflect: what impact have the strategies had that you can identify?

After you have trialled your new strategies and approach to effective stretch and challenge, it is vital that you reflect on the impact on the students' achievement. You will need to look again at a range of data to help you identify which strategies to continue with and which strategies did not work as well as you had hoped for; take time to consider why a particular strategy or approach did not work out as you expected.

- What changes have you identified in the student(s)' participation in lessons?
- What feedback have the students given about the strategies?
- What feedback have the students' families given about any changes they have noticed?
- Do the students' assessments show any improvement?

Tweak: how will you adapt your use of strategies now you have reflected on their initial impact?

The final stage of the cycle is important as this could make the difference between short-term impact and long-term embedded change. You will have reflected on how your students responded to the new strategies and approaches. Now it is time to tweak the strategies you had most success with and consider what small, practical and manageable changes you can make so that your stretch and challenge provision becomes even better.

- Which strategies have worked best and why?
- Which strategies didn't work as well and why?
- Are you going to implement all of the strategies in the same way or use them differently?

Scenario 1: A high-achieving class who work hard and enjoy learning

Diagnose

- Latest progress data shows all students are on track to make good progress.
- Behaviour for learning is excellent and students have excellent attitudes to learning.
- Homework is always completed.
- Students are quiet and like to get on with their work individually.
- Students are not keen on working in groups.
- Whole-class discussions are a challenge as students are fairly quiet.

Plan

To increase their level of challenge so students experience learning that is suitably challenging and requires students to come out of their comfort zone.

- Strategy 1: Philosophy for Children (page 60) – the teacher introduces regular sessions of P4C with the aim of facilitating learning as opposed to leading it. A rota is used to ensure different members of the class lead the debate. The sessions should encourage students to apply their knowledge to higher-order thinking questions which are different to the questions they are used to in their usual textbook that is used in class. This should increase their knowledge by using it in different contexts.
- Strategy 7 Public presentation (page 62) – the teacher sets up a schedule for students to present their homework to the rest of the class. If students know that they not only have to complete their homework but also share their thinking with their peers, this should increase the level of challenge. Students will need to think carefully about how they will present their knowledge in an engaging and interactive way and also be prepared to take questions from the class. This should challenge students to see what knowledge they draw upon when they do not have a pre-prepared response.
- Strategy 8 Desirable difficulties (page 63) – the teacher decides to introduce a new idea with students at the end of each cycle of four lessons. This idea brings into question what the students think is true. Students are given half an hour in small groups of three to answer the question: 'Now you know this new information, how does this affect your understanding?' Students are given time to access resources before sharing their new understanding with the rest of the class. Groups that have differences of opinion then debate what they think they know and the teacher does not get involved until the end of the lesson.
- Strategy 29 Find and share excellence (page 75) – students are given a project which lasts the whole half term, and the aim of the project is to research an expert in the field they are studying. The teacher asks the students: 'How did this person become an expert in their field?' Students have to consider what contribution the expert has made to the field as well as how they become an expert. At the end of the half term, students create a three-minute video to watch with the rest of the class on their chosen expert.

Reflect

The teacher reflected on the impact of the strategies implemented and concluded the following:

- Students enjoyed the opportunity to think about the bigger picture and move away from the textbook.
- Students said they would not always want to learn using oral methods such as 'Public presentation' or 'Philosophy for Children' but they believed it had taken

them out of their comfort zone and given them a chance to apply their knowledge in a way they weren't used to. They agreed they would like to build in these opportunities but still engage in individual written work for most of the time.

- Students reported that they enjoyed the research task for homework and would like to continue with these types of research projects in the future.

The teacher tested the students at the end of the term and only one student did not reach the expected standard and four of the students made more than expected progress.

Tweak

The teacher felt that introducing 'Desirable difficulties' had not had as much impact as they had hoped. Students had mixed reactions to this new strategy. Some students felt it was counterproductive to not share all the information at once and felt almost tricked. Others enjoyed having their ideas tested and worked well in their groups to rethink their understanding. The teacher felt that students needed more guidance in accessing resources in the time they had to formulate their new response after introducing the desirable difficulty. More careful thought needed to be given to the resources students had as many of them weren't able to go beyond making basic connections between their prior learning and the new information.

If you have a class like this in which students are used to finding learning quite easy and their attitudes to learning are generally positive, then these strategies might work for you. The chosen strategies are about trying to take the students out of their comfort zone – working quietly and individually to complete their work. These strategies encourage them to think more deeply, to be given more time for serious reflection and to build deeper connections between different learning episodes. The stretch and challenge approaches that can work well for a class like this are developing students' independence and ability to engage in discussion.

Scenario 2: A coasting top set

Diagnose

- Students think of themselves as clever because they are in a top set.
- They have not had to struggle and don't feel they have to work particularly hard to achieve.
- Students often do the bare minimum in class and are more interested in finishing work quickly rather than producing anything of real quality.
- Homework is completed but any real effort at home is saved for revision for tests they consider important.
- Data suggests that most students are on track to achieve but few are accelerating.
- The attitude of the students is to be focused on grades rather than learning.

Plan

To increase the students' appetite for learning and to encourage them to take greater responsibility for developing their own learning.

- Strategy 4 Examples of excellence (page 61) – the teacher creates a bank of exemplars using past students' essays for the topic students are studying. The teacher has decided that the students are going to write one timed essay a fortnight that term and students are shown an example of excellence before beginning their own essay. The teacher leads the students in discussing what made the essay an example of excellence. From this discussion, students and teacher co-construct success criteria for the timed essay that fortnight.
- Strategy 10 Generative learning (page 64) – the teacher scrutinises their current scheme of work to identify the core concepts to be taught that term. After establishing what the core concepts are for the scheme of work, the teacher constructs questions for students to answer in small groups before introducing them to the new core concept linked to the questions. These generative learning sessions last for 15 minutes before the teacher then spends the rest of the lesson sharing the new core concept and then students return to the initial question to answer.
- Strategy 12 Ownership of feedback (page 66) – the teacher shares this new strategy with students, making it clear that students would not be receiving any new feedback on their work until they could prove they had closed their learning gaps from the previous work. Students are given a choice in how they could demonstrate that they had closed their learning gaps; either students could annotate their essays, highlighting changes they had made based on the teacher's feedback, or they could redo the essay from scratch.
- Strategy 35 Pose big questions (page 78) – the teacher sets aside a week before each half-term break to pose a big question that would enable students to draw upon the knowledge they had learnt that half term. The question is linked to current topical issues and students would not just be able to regurgitate knowledge from class but would also need to make connections between them and carry out further research. The outcome is that students have to work in groups to present their response to the big question to the rest of the class once they return from the half-term break to give them enough time to carry out further study out of class time.

Reflect

The teacher reflected on the impact of the strategies implemented and concluded the following:

- Students responded well to seeing and discussing examples of excellence. Many of the students were surprised at what was expected of them if they were to produce something at the top of the mark scheme.

- Students acknowledged that whilst they were achieving some of the mark scheme, there was further work to do on their essays if they were to achieve the top grade. Linked to this, students' attitudes to their work improved through strategy 12 'Ownership of feedback' as now students were clear on what they needed to do to produce excellent work.
- At first, there was some lethargy in students' evidencing that they were closing their learning gaps and annotations were limited. However, once the handful of students realised that the teacher was not going to give any further feedback until the students' response to feedback was of an appropriate quality, students took these reflection sessions seriously.

Tweak

The teacher was not prepared for students to disengage from the generative learning sessions. Many students complained they couldn't create an informed response as they didn't have all of the information. The students weren't resilient enough to deal with knowing what to do when you don't know something. Therefore, the teacher decided that this strategy would have to be put on hold until the students' attitude to learning improved and they had developed more robust learning habits. The strategy of posing big questions had some positive impact on students as they all had opportunities to make connections between the knowledge they had learnt over the half term; however, not all students took the opportunity to deepen their knowledge by engaging in further study outside of the classroom and carry out further research, meaning some of the group presentations lacked depth. The teacher decided to continue with posing big questions but tweak the criteria to make it much more explicit what the expectation was with regards to what extra research the teacher expected to see evidenced in the presentation.

These strategies are very useful if you are looking to experiment with your approach to feedback and discussion to develop students' independence. If you have students or a whole class who are coasting and not putting in maximum effort then feedback can play an important role in raising their expectations of what quality work looks like. Asking students to close their own learning gaps by using the feedback they've been given ensures students are taking responsibility for their own learning, which stops students from coasting and expecting the teacher to work harder than them. It is telling that coasting students find generative learning difficult as it requires resilience and independent thought; focusing on this approach should help these students to push forward with their learning.

Scenario 3: The invisible child

Diagnose

- The student is very quiet and prefers to work alone as he feels uncomfortable working in groups.

- He completes his work but does not attempt any of the more challenging tasks due to a lack of confidence.
- He refuses to participate in any whole-class discussion as he doesn't like the spotlight to be put on him and prefers to say he doesn't know or he's forgotten what he was going to say.
- He does not like to ask the teacher or his peers any questions at the risk of looking silly in front of them.
- Data shows the student is at risk of not achieving; parents say he has always been shy and that's just his personality.

Plan

To develop the student's confidence in group and whole-class settings and establish routines to make questioning and discussion an effective way for him to learn.

- Strategy 3 Devil's advocate (page 60) – the teacher establishes a routine in which students have one starter a week which is discussion based. The teacher writes a statement on the board and students work in pairs to argue both sides of the statement. The targeted student is given a cue card during these discussion starters. On the card, the teacher has given hints and key words for the student to use to present the counter-argument to his peer's argument.
- Strategy 17 Right is right - oral rehearsal (page 70) – in the same pairs used for the previous strategy, in order to build familiarity and confidence with each other, students are given time to practise their responses before committing their ideas to paper. The targeted student must speak for two minutes without any interruption from his partner. Once he has verbally rehearsed his response, his partner then gives him feedback on how to improve. The teacher reiterates the principle that all feedback is kind, helpful and specific. The student then has a second attempt at rehearsing their response.
- Strategy 33 Peer support (page 77) – the teacher once again keeps the same pairings to activate peer support. The teacher begins with an accessible strategy: 'think, pair, share'. The targeted student is used to working by himself and the teacher identifies that this strategy still allows him time to think quietly before then listening to the ideas of his peer. The teacher decides not to force the student to contribute when the two pairs merge into a four to share and evaluate all the ideas before sharing their best idea and prefers to gently encourage the student in private to share in the group of four once they have got comfortable using 'think, pair, share'.

Reflect

The teacher reflected on the impact of the strategies implemented and concluded the following:

- There was a significant change in the student's participation in class – so much so that other teachers commented on his increased confidence in their classes.

- The teacher judged the needs of their student well and realised the success of these strategies would lie with incremental steps toward increased participation. Not all strategies were implemented at the same time.
- The teacher only used 'Devil's advocate' for the first month to help the student to build a relationship with his peer through these starter activities. Once the student experienced success with Devil's advocate, the teacher then began activating peer support in the main body of the lesson.
- The teacher waited half a term before introducing 'Right is right - oral rehearsal' to the pairing; by this time, the targeted student had stopped being the 'invisible child' and had found his voice.

By the end of the term when the student was formally assessed, his work showed a dramatic improvement with regards to quality of ideas and a reduction in the number of careless errors.

Tweak

The teacher delayed introducing 'Right is right - oral rehearsal' to the pairing until the end of the term. As a result, this strategy was less well used in comparison to the other two strategies. One thing the teacher noticed when standing close to the students when they were practising 'Right is right - oral rehearsal' was that the targeted student's peer seemed more concerned with being nice to him rather than give him constructive feedback on his initial response. All students in the class were told to stick to the 'Kind, helpful and specific' principle but the feedback given by his peer was not specific enough to support the student to make quality amendments to their initial response; therefore, the second attempt was not much different from the initial attempt. The teacher decided that next term she would continue to use 'Right is right - oral rehearsal' but create laminated cards with identified areas for improvement and suggested feedback students could give to scaffold the feedback more effectively.

If you have an 'invisible child' in any of your classes then the approach you need to consider is how you group your students. You can be using a range of excellent strategies but if the student doesn't have the confidence to engage, then the impact will be minimal. Spend time deciding on who is an effective peer to place the invisible child with so that they can support each other's learning. Once the groupings have been set up effectively, the focus on vocabulary and oracy is an important approach to develop as this will link to the students' level of confidence in your class.

Scenario 4: A disengaged, low-achieving group of students

Diagnose

- Students consider themselves as failures as they are in a bottom set.
- Students rarely complete work in lessons and do not engage with homework.

- Students prefer to be passive and enjoy it when the teacher spoon-feeds them.
- Behaviour in lessons can be a challenge; students can either act up to distract from the fact they are not able to do the work or withdraw completely.
- Students will only work with other students they consider to be their friends but there is often a lot of off-task talking.

Plan

To support students by providing opportunities for them to experience success with their learning and encourage them to become more resilient when they find things difficult.

- Strategy 9 Frequent, low-stakes quizzes (page 64) – the teacher decides to use frequent, low-stakes quizzes as an alternative to the usual end-of-topic test for two reasons. Firstly, the students are completely put off by the pressure of a big test at the end of the topic and have refused to sit the test in the past. This has a considerable impact on their progress data as it does not always reflect accurately what the students know. Secondly, the students often say that they understand something they are being taught but when it comes to the end of topic test, they have either forgotten it or overestimated how much they really did understand of what they were being taught. Consequently, the teacher creates a ten question quiz at the end of each fortnight to judge how much the students have learnt. As the quizzes progress, the teacher includes questions from previous weeks to encourage students to draw upon their long-term memory. Students are rewarded with a phone call home if they get at least 80 percent on the quizzes.
- Strategy 11 Student learning audit (page 65) – the teacher creates an audit for students to complete in which they reflect on the skills they need to be successful in the subject and consider where they have used these skills. The teacher then talks with each student individually (the teacher is able to do this as there are only 14 students in the class) whilst the rest of the class are working on a task set by the teacher. During this conversation, the teacher works with the student to set a target for the student to work on a particular skill and identify specific opportunities for how they could show they are working on this skill.
- Strategy 14 Find and fix errors (page 67) – the teacher selects one student's work each lesson and types it up onto a PowerPoint slide to share with the rest of the class. In pairs, students are given a specific focus when reading the student's work; they must come up to the board and show where in the piece of work they would make a change. By the end of the term, nearly all students in the class have had their work looked at by the whole class and received feedback. Once the individual student has received feedback from the class, their homework for that week is to rewrite their answer using the annotations made by the students at the board.

- Strategy 28 Group accountability (page 74) – the teacher is keen to teach the students how to work in groups effectively. The teacher has tried group work in the past but has been put off by the off-task behaviour and reverted to getting students to complete work by themselves or occasionally in pairs. The teacher thinks carefully about what type of task would warrant students working collaboratively together. The teacher decides to create an end-of-topic display; each group is given a different aspect of the display to work on. There are two groups of three and two groups of four; each person in the group is given a specific role and told that if they do not contribute, then the group will be unable to produce their piece for display. The roles assigned are: researcher (two researchers in the groups of four, each looking at a different stimulus), designer (producer of the display piece) and resource collector (the student wins extra resources based on questions they answer correctly).

Reflect

The teacher reflected on the impact of the strategies implemented and concluded the following:

- The students really got on board with the frequent quizzes instead of the more formal end-of-topic test. At first, the students' scores were quite low but the teacher decided to display all of their scores on a leader board. Although this was a risky move and could further alienate students, it was thought that this competitive edge would work for this particular group of learners. After a couple more tests, students' scores started to rise and the students enjoyed receiving positive phone calls home once they started hitting the 80 percent mark. Students wanted to beat their friends and began to motivate each other to use their homework to revise the content of what they had been studying.
- The learning audit was a longer-term goal and more of a tool for reflection than something that would have instant impact on the students' progress. At the end of the term, the teacher wrote a mini report home to each parent detailing what target the student had set for themselves based on the learning audit and examples of where the student had shown an improvement. It worked as a great motivator.

Tweak

The 'Find and fix errors' strategy was a success and improved the students' ability to deconstruct their work and find ways to improve but the first couple of times the teacher tried to use this strategy were not successful. The students did not like having their work selected to display on the board; they felt exposed and their behaviour became quite defiant. As a result, some of the students in the group felt reluctant to identify the errors and offer improvements. In hindsight, the teacher felt they could have started out using work that wasn't the students to make them feel more comfortable critiquing work. However, after a few attempts, the students were much more capable of critiquing work and by the end of the term, a routine had been firmly embedded. With regards to improving their group work, the display at the end of the topic was an effective way of developing these crucial collaborative skills and increasing their accountability as well as visibly celebrating the work the students were now able to do. The teacher decided to continue this group display activity at the end of each half term.

If you have a group of disaffected learners, then groupings and the use of feedback should be your priorities. Disaffected learners tend to feed off each other's negative learning behaviours, so helping to work together is an important step forward. Once students have formed good learning habits, then they will be ready to use feedback to challenge themselves to improve their learning. Get the environment right first; otherwise, the students will not be in the right frame of mind to take any feedback on board.

Scenario 5: A group of students with low levels of literacy in a mixed-ability class

Diagnose

- Data shows the group of students are at risk of underachieving as they struggle to access a range of texts and to express themselves coherently on paper and in discussion.
- These students dislike asking for help as they don't want to draw attention to their literacy needs.
- The students have learnt to disguise their needs by copying from other students or pretending to read without following the text.
- Their writing reveals there is some understanding but the students' power of expression hinders their progress.
- Students will participate in class discussion but can often struggle to extend their responses into full sentences and can sometimes switch between registers.

Plan
To boost the students' reading, writing and speaking through a clear focus on vocabulary development which will lead to them gaining confidence in their literacy.

- Strategy 18 Stretch it - upgrade initial responses (page 70) – the teacher decides to focus on improving students' use of vocabulary and to extend their responses by including the word 'because' when explaining their thinking. The teacher targets questions at the group of students with low levels of literacy. Students are not allowed to respond for ten seconds whilst they construct in their minds their initial answer. The teacher then invites one student to share their response before asking other students to select a word that they could upgrade. The teacher returns to the student and asks them to repeat their answer but this time with the vocabulary upgrades. The teacher then repeats the process but with a focus on using the word 'because' to extend the explanation. By the end, the student has a developed and coherent response to the teacher's question. The teacher keeps track in their planning which students from the group of learners have upgraded their responses each week.

- Strategy 23 Vocabulary notebooks (page 72) – the teacher hands out A5 vocabulary notebooks and the students divide each page into different boxes: a box for a description of the word; an example sentence using the word; synonyms; antonyms; a visual representation of the word. When they commence using the vocabulary book, the work is scaffolded so that the teacher has completed most of the boxes but as the term goes on, the teacher fills in fewer boxes as the students become more familiar using the vocabulary notebook. Every fortnight, the students have a vocabulary test in which they have to use the words in context to prove they have remembered their meaning.

- Strategy 24 Vocabulary upgrade (page 72) – in combination with strategy 23, the teacher has a reading focus for 20 minutes each week. The teacher selects a passage to read as a whole class and highlights several words which are easy words that students would know. The challenge is for students to replace these words and phrases with tier 2 more mature words or tier 3 more technical language. At the start of implementing this strategy, the teacher allows students to use their notebooks to remind them of the key words they have been learning; however, as students progress with their vocabulary and become more familiar with the words as they are consolidated, the teacher encourages the students to upgrade the words and phrases without using the notebooks.

- Strategy 25 Vocabulary games revision (page 72) – the teacher incorporates opportunities at the end of lessons for recalling vocabulary through a series of literacy games. The teacher uses the game Taboo in which students have to describe a word without using the easy words on the banned list. In addition, the teacher uses the odd one out game when focusing on tier 3 words to encourage students to make connections between the technical vocabulary and consider how to categorise these words.

- Strategy 36 Ask 'Why?' (page 79) – when the students encounter an extended text to read, the teacher pre-reads it and identifies the key points the students need to understand. The teacher displays the text but does not show it all at once to make sure the students are not put off by reading such a large amount of text. Once the teacher has chunked the reading onto different slides, the teacher has two 'Why?' questions for each slide and the students pause for a few minutes to discuss in pairs what they think. The students then note down their responses to the 'Why?' questions. At the end, the teacher then hands out the full text and reads it aloud to the students in full without stopping so the students can gain a sense of how ideas in the text develop.

Reflect

The teacher reflected on the impact of the strategies implemented and concluded the following:

- The students with low literacy levels made excellent progress due to these strategies; in their test, which involved reading two passages and answering a series of comprehension questions, students' answers were significantly better than their previous test. Students' use of vocabulary in their answers had improved as had their use of the word 'because' to increase the level of detail in their explanations.
- Students liked adding words to their vocabulary notebooks and commented that including antonyms as well as synonyms helped them to remember the meaning of the words. Parents were also encouraged to go over the words with their children before each fortnightly vocabulary test.
- The use of literacy games to reinforce the meaning of challenging words and to make connections between them proved very effective in consolidating the students' learning.

Tweak

The teacher acknowledged that the strategies chosen were quite labour intensive and had increased their planning time because they had to create the sheets for the vocabulary notebooks and find the words to upgrade in the passages they read as a class. The teacher's next step was to ensure the students took responsibility for their vocabulary notebooks now that they were confident using them as part of their routine. The teacher would now only need to provide the word and the description of its meaning, whilst the students would complete the other parts of the notebook. In a similar way, the teacher wanted to build up a greater independence in the students so they were able to identify the easier words that could be upgraded in the passages selected for reading and also begin to create their own 'Why?' questions when chunking the text. The teacher's aim moving forward is to make it automatic for students to draw upon these literacy strategies when reading, writing and speaking.

If you are teaching students with low levels of literacy, they will really struggle to access the curriculum. As a result, the approach to take would be to develop how you teach vocabulary. If students are unable to speak using the correct academic language or are unable to read texts because they are unfamiliar with the more sophisticated vocabulary, then their progress will be limited. Regardless of what subject you teach, ensure you set aside plenty of opportunities to teach vocabulary that your students will need to access your content.

Scenario 6: A co-dependent pair of students who are achieving but not accelerating

Diagnose

- Students perform moderately well in formal assessments but put little effort into learning during lesson time.
- Students focus on making their work look presentable at the expense of improving their work.
- They will only work with each other; when challenged to work with other peers, they withdraw from the tasks.
- When they are allowed to work together, they often end up chatting rather than supporting each other's learning.
- They don't challenge each other for fear of upsetting each other.

Plan

To develop more productive learning habits in the two students so they are able to support and challenge one another to make better progress with their learning.

- Strategy 6 Peer critique (page 62) – the teacher has identified that the two students are not making the most of reflection and feedback tasks. The teacher has used WWW (What Went Well) and EBI (Even Better If) with the class but the quality of the two students' feedback suggests they are not getting much from the process – comments are vague at best and targets are unrealistic. The teacher decides to change the way she plans for peer assessment and instead uses peer critique. The students are given two coloured highlighters. One colour is used to highlight a strength of their peer's work using the success criteria. The student has to justify why they have selected this particular part of the work. The process is repeated using the other colour and focusing on a part of the work that does not fully meet the criteria. At the end, the students are not allowed to hand back the highlighted work without verbally explaining to their peer why they have chosen these parts of their work. They also get their peer to commit to an action they will carry out to develop their work. This is written down and shared with the teacher.
- Strategy 16 Deliberate practice RAG checklist (page 68) – in their current topic, the teacher has created three formal assessment opportunities. In order to reduce the passivity in the targeted students, the teacher has created a checklist of everything the students should include in their assessment. The students are asked to RAG the checklist – red for unconfident, amber for OK but needs a bit more work and green for covered in depth. The teacher then uses the information from the RAG checklist to put students into pairs where there is a similar area for development so they can work together to improve their red and amber areas by completing set tasks before handing in their assessment. Once the students have made amendments to their assessments,

they hand in the assessment with the attached RAG checklist so the teacher can see to what extent the students have taken responsibility for improving their own work as well as supporting others.

- Strategy 34 Students design their own tests (page 78) – the teacher decides to set a considerable challenge for the pair of codependent students by making them create a test for each other to take at the end of the topic. The teacher shares with them what they are expected to know and cover in the test. The students then have the whole lesson to construct the test as well as the accompanying personalised mark scheme. The next lesson, the students take each other's test and then they have to mark each other's work using the mark scheme they have created for their test.

Reflect

The teacher reflected on the impact of the strategies implemented and concluded the following:

- The biggest success is the switch from the WWW/EBI peer assessment to the more structured peer critique. Regardless of whether the students are worried about offending each other, the peer critique approach holds each other to account as they have to set an action to complete after receiving the feedback. The actions are realistic and measurable and the teacher makes the students responsible for checking that their peer has completed their action. The level of accountability and responsibility has clearly increased in comparison to lessons before using this strategy.
- The RAG checklist was also a useful visible reminder to the two students about what is expected of each other's work. In the past when they would have missed parts of the mark scheme, they still would have handed in their assessments but now they are working together to help each other close their learning gaps and hence receive an improved score.

Tweak

Although the two students took seriously designing a test for each other, the teacher realised that she had underestimated how difficult the students found this task. Some of the questions on the test were too easy or worded in such a way that they could be misleading for their peer. The teacher wanted to try out this strategy again but decided more careful modelling was required in order to show the students what was expected of them and to ensure that students were able to show what they had learnt as too many of the questions were lower order. The teacher considered using a question matrix as a resource to support students in ensuring that they created a test which stretched the student to tackle more difficult questions.

If you are teaching students who seem to be doing quite well and making some progress, then these students could fall to the side as you concentrate on more high profile students who may be at risk of not achieving. Yet we need to make sure that all students have the chance to achieve well. Focusing on learning intentions and subsequent success criteria is key to challenging middle-achieving students to accelerate their learning. Making the learning explicit and showing students the steps to success will help them navigate through more challenging learning.

Scenario 7: An enthusiastic class where students lack the self-discipline to achieve their best

Diagnose

- Students enjoy whole-class discussion but can often go off on a tangent and louder students tend to dominate.
- Work generally gets completed but not always to the expected standard.
- After receiving feedback on work, students don't really engage and often make the same mistakes in the next assessment.
- Data shows that most students are on track to achieve but there are a handful of students who are at risk of not achieving well.
- Homework records show patchy completion rates and parents have been contacted several times to encourage students to complete work at home.

Plan

To create a more structured and disciplined learning environment so students' enthusiasm translates into accelerated achievement.

- Strategy 2 Socratic discussion (page 60) – the teacher replaces the class's usual discussion routines with Socratic discussion in pairs. The teacher sets aside half an hour every three lessons for the discussion to take place; fifteen minutes is for paired discussion and then a further fifteen minutes for the teacher to share some of the more interesting ideas based on going around the class and listening to what students are saying to each other. This approach is more structured, and by having the students discuss in pairs rather than as a whole class, means all students have to participate. Moreover, the questions students have to ask each other as part of the Socratic discussion means it is less likely for particular students to dominate or for others to go off on a tangent.
- Strategy 5 Redrafting process (page 61) – the teacher has complained in the past of students handing in work that is not a true reflection of what the students are capable of and has found it frustrating marking work which is littered with careless errors or undeveloped points. The teacher explains to the students that instead of completing two pieces of unconnected work this term, they will work on redrafting one, more challenging piece of work until it becomes an excellent example of work. The teacher continues to teach the

topic in the same way but the only difference is that the students spend ten minutes at the end of each lesson refining their piece of work based on new information they have gained that lesson. The teacher routinely takes in the same piece of work at the end of each lesson and offers just one piece of feedback that they want the student to do the following week.

- Strategy 20 A set of task instructions (page 71) – the teacher decides that some of the students in the group who can easily go off task would benefit from a clear set of instructions that they can tick off as they work. The targeted students often make a good start but run out of steam and either rush their work or end up repeating themselves. As the term progresses, the teacher withdraws the use of the set of instructions for some of the students but not all of them. When the targeted students are using the set of task instructions, they have to attach these instructions to their work so the teacher can see whether they are making effective use of them.
- Strategy 31 Set and reflect on targets (page 76) – students would normally be set one homework per week but the teacher decides to change this and set one homework slot a fortnight. Each student is asked to reflect on their learning that fortnight and the feedback they have received from the teacher and their peers. Based on this reflection, each student sets themselves a homework task from a bank of options. The first fifteen minutes of the new fortnightly cycle is given over to students sharing with their group what they have done and how this has closed their learning gaps.
- Strategy 32 Preflight checklists (page 77) – the teacher incorporates this strategy alongside strategy 5 'Redrafting process' to encourage students to take greater accountability for each other's work. During the topic, the teacher builds in three preflight checklist opportunities where feedback buddies (the same pairings used for Socratic discussion) go through the class checklist for the redrafted piece of work and highlight to their peer what is missing still or what needs further development.

Reflect

The teacher reflected on the impact of the strategies implemented and concluded the following:

- The biggest change that the teacher identified in terms of impact was the sense of purpose in their classroom. Before, time was wasted and this affected the students' outcomes. Even though the students were generally enthusiastic and wanted to learn, they didn't always follow through.

- By making the commitment to work on just one assessment over many weeks, the students really began to take pride in this piece of work and wanted it to be the best thing they'd ever produced. The structured time at the end of each lesson to work on their piece combined with the checklists and target setting heightened the students' sense of responsibility for their own work.

Tweak

The Socratic discussion was an effective addition to the lessons but not all of the pairings worked. The teacher concluded that some of the pairings found it difficult to discuss for an extended period of time and that not all of the students' personalities were well matched. A rejigging of the pairings would need to happen if Socratic discussion continued to be a feature of the teacher's class. The setting of targets and using homework to close the learning gaps was a partial success but not all of the students did their homework, which meant they had little to contribute to the follow-up group discussion the next lesson. The teacher now knew which students may not do the homework and would plan for those students to come out of the groups and complete set tasks directed by the teacher.

If you have a group of students who have good attitudes to learning but struggle to apply themselves, then focusing on groupings, useful resources and homework could support them to become more effective learners. By structuring group tasks so that the students stay in the same pairs and have prompts and scaffolds, enables students to make progress more quickly. High-quality scaffolds such as checklists and a structured series of questions means there is no reason for students to go off task. Focusing on homework as a key aspect of your stretch and challenge provision also helps students to realise that you have high expectations of them both in and outside of the classroom.

Scenario 8: A student who has difficulties in processing information and memory retention

Diagnose

- Data shows that the student has a long history of underachievement despite having a positive attitude to learning.
- The parents are worried about their child's future as they can't understand why teachers say the student is working well in class but yet does so poorly in test conditions.
- The student generally performs poorly in tests if there is a requirement to apply knowledge in a different format to what they have worked on previously.
- The student struggles to make connections between prior and current learning.
- The student believes they have understood new information but when asked to articulate their new understanding, they struggle to give a coherent response.
- The student often participates with enthusiasm during lessons but struggles to remember what they have learnt in subsequent lessons, which can cause anxiety.

Plan

To boost the student's memory and support them to make connections between prior and current learning so they are able to see the bigger picture.

- Strategy 22 Model and describe (page 71) – the teacher has created a positive learning environment in which students are able to work independently if they are provided with good-quality scaffolds. As a result, this frees up the teacher to sit with the particular student and model for her how to go about completing tasks. One of the main issues is the student's inability to make connections between different pieces of knowledge, so the teacher models for the student what questions they should be asking to complete the task and verbally describes each step they do of the task. The student watches carefully how the teacher completes the task before trying to complete it for themselves.
- Strategy 26 Mind maps (page 74) – to support the student in seeing the bigger picture of what she is going to learn during this topic, the teacher creates a mind map template. On strips of paper, the teacher writes down key pieces of knowledge and asks the student to place them on the mind map to show how they connect. At the end of each lesson, the student adds one or two new pieces of information to their mind map and begins to use colour to highlight connections.
- Strategy 27 Revisit threshold concepts (page 74) – combined with strategy 26 'Mind maps', each week the teacher builds in time to revisit one of the threshold concepts that has already been covered earlier in the topic. By the end of the term, the class have experienced the threshold concepts several times but in different ways – video clips, class discussion, writing tasks, reading different texts and homework. The teacher uses frequent short tests but includes questions from much earlier in the topic to encourage the student to draw upon their long-term memory and strengthen the neural connections.
- Strategy 37 Knowledge organisers (page 79) – the student sometimes doesn't complete the same tasks as others in the class. Every lesson, the class is asked to complete a written response to evidence what they have learnt that lesson; however, the student is asked to replace some of these writing tasks with creating knowledge organisers instead. The teacher has provided a template for the student to complete and it is the size of a page of A4. The knowledge organiser includes: key words; space to write a short paragraph using the key words; a higher order thinking question; space to include resources and websites to aid revision; a red flag to highlight misconceptions the student has had when learning the topic.
- Strategy 38 Plan for forgetting (page 79) – the teacher identifies from the data alongside discussion with the student, which aspects of the learning they have found most difficult over the past few weeks. A homework session is planned so that the student returns to prior work and watches videos on an educational YouTube channel to remind them of crucial learning. The teacher gives the

students a series of test questions to answer which she will be able to do once she has watched the recommended videos.

Reflect

The teacher reflected on the impact of the strategies implemented and concluded the following:

- The recommended videos on the YouTube channel had a strong effect on the student's ability to remember information required for assessments. The student reported that she liked the videos because she could pause them and watch them repeatedly. By following this up with completing the teacher's quiz before the formal assessment, the student said it gave her greater confidence.
- Linked to this, the student's use of graphic organisers proved valuable for repackaging information and supporting memory retention.

Tweak

When the teacher discussed with the student what the core threshold concepts were for the term, the student didn't seem clear about how they built on each other. Making connections between the learning was still a struggle even though her memory retention had improved. The teacher felt that greater attention needed to be given to the mind-mapping process as the student found it increasingly difficult to use it effectively when a considerable amount of information was put on it. The teacher would need to show the student examples of mind maps to demonstrate how they work when populated with lots of interconnected information.

If you teach students who have poor memory retention, then you will need to make the learning even more explicit. This ties in with focusing your approach on learning intentions and use of resources to make content memorable. Students with poor memory retention will struggle to make connections so the way you frame and share learning intentions is crucial. Building up quality resources, such as scaffold, videos and quiz questions takes time, but it is worth investing time with this approach to stretch and challenge if you are teaching students who will need that extra input into helping them remember what they have been taught in class.

Scenario 9: A small group of students in a mixed-ability class who are making some progress but lack the confidence to work independently

Diagnose

- Students hate getting things wrong and will often wait for the teacher to give the right answer rather than try and work things out for themselves.

- Students have a negative response to constructive criticism and can sometimes withdraw from tasks.
- Students thrive on praise and put in lots of effort once they have received praise from the teacher.
- Students can find it difficult to get started unless the teacher is nearby.
- There is an over-reliance on the TA who works with this group to write things for them or give them the answers.

Plan

To increase students' ability to work independently and accept that making mistakes offers opportunities for further learning.

- Strategy 13 Reinforce growth mindset through homework (page 66) – the students are reminded of the key skills they were working on in last term's scheme of work. The students rank these skills in terms of how confident they are in applying these skills. The skill they are least confident in using becomes the focus of their homework for the next month. Students have to revise and practise this skill by completing the task given to them by the teacher. Once they have practised their least-confident skill, they then create a visually appealing resource to help other students practise.
- Strategy 15 Help desk (page 68) – the teacher changes their scheme of work to include a mini project that students complete in groups. The four students who struggle to work independently are put together in the same group and given a range of resources that they can use if they wish. Each student in the group can visit the help desk for a resource but only one student at a time. They only get one visit per lesson and have to make their decision after five minutes and go back to their group. The group has to complete an additional task which is to rate the usefulness of each resource they used to complete their mini project.
- Strategy 21 Shorten the feedback loop (page 71) – based on diagnosing these students' needs, the teacher recognises that the students are not yet ready to self-assess their work in any great depth. They are still too reliant on the teacher's input and that of the TA. As a bridge to setting up effective feedback models, the teacher looks at the students' work but rather than giving them individual feedback, the teacher collates their errors and tells them how to fix them. Students read their work again and make three simple changes to their work based on the errors the teacher found.
- Strategy 30 Learning wall (page 76) – to boost this group of students' confidence, the teacher asks them to look back at their work and select a piece that they want to refine and include on the class learning wall. This process is one way of supporting students to acknowledge that no work is perfect and improvements can always be made. Having the work displayed on the wall fosters a sense of pride and encourages them to put in greater effort to

improving their identified piece of work. The teacher does not work directly with the students when they are improving their identified piece apart from providing the students with a series of reflection questions.

Reflect

The teacher reflected on the impact of the strategies implemented and concluded the following:

- The students really enjoyed the challenge of creating useful resources for each other as part of their homework to revise skills they found difficult first time around. The students created knowledge organisers and annotated worked examples to support each other.
- As well as more effort shown in homework, the students also responded well to the teacher shortening the feedback loop and working together in their small group to spot errors in their own work and read other's work. As all of them had errors to fix, no one felt isolated and instead errors were seen as a normal part of the learning process.
- The use of the 'Learning wall' encouraged the students to approach their work with a different mindset; they were able to acknowledge that there were good features in their work but knew that they couldn't include their work on the class wall until they had worked hard to develop it further. This was a good example of the students' resilience and independence.

Tweak

Students still need to work on their self-regulation and this was evident from how they responded to the help desk. The teacher had included some really useful resources which the students didn't even bother picking up because they looked too hard. They still went for the easiest resources rather than pushing themselves to engage with something more challenging. Moreover, the four students still asked for the teacher's and TA's help frequently despite being told they would not be able to ask anything for a period of fifteen minutes to encourage them to use the resources provided instead. The teacher will adapt this strategy by including question tokens to minimise the amount of questions the students ask; the visual reminder that they only have a set number of question tokens should make them think more carefully about when they use up their tokens.

If you teach a group of students who lack the confidence to work independently, then you should focus your approaches on how to boost their confidence and become familiar with taking responsibility for their own learning. These particular strategies focus on placing the emphasis on the students doing more than the teacher. The teacher's role is more to support students in identifying areas of improvement and working with them to close these learning gaps. Getting students to act on feedback, work together in groups to support each other and scaffold the learning experiences through a series of reflection questions are all effective strategies in challenging students to increase their independence in class.

Chapter 5 takeaway

Teaching tip
Connect with other schools
When you think you've done something really well in your own school, look out and see what other schools are doing; you can always learn from others and magpie some of their ideas. Never think that what you've done can't be improved. We need to role model to our students that learning is a continuous process.

Pass it on
Invite another school to come in and do a learning walk on a particular department or aspect of pedagogy the whole school has been working on. Before the learning walk takes place, be clear with the other school what your vision is, what the current reality is, the changes you've been trying to implement and the impact you think you can see. Ask for honest feedback from those conducting the learning walk as we're all guilty of tunnel vision when we work on something for extended periods and want it to be a success.

Share and tweet
Share your experiences of working with other schools on Twitter using the hashtag #BloomsCPD.

CPD book club recommendation
Geoff Petty's *Evidence-Based Teaching* is an excellent read for teachers interested in how research can shape our practice. (See Bibliography and further reading, page 273)

Bloggers' corner
Rachel Jones' blog on student learning and the role technology can play in challenging students to be creative with their learning is a fascinating read. Visit her blog at: createinnovateexplore.com.

To do list:

- ❏ Invite colleagues from another school to carry out a learning walk and get the benefit of a fresh pair of eyes
- ❏ Tweet your experiences of school-to-school collaboration using the hashtag #BloomsCPD
- ❏ Check out Rachel Jones' blog on using technology to enhance student learning: createinnovateexplore.com
- ❏ Read *Evidence-Based Teaching* by Geoff Petty

6

Self-evaluation and reflection

At this point, you should have spent some time trialing new strategies or refining a particular approach to stretch and challenge. Now it is time to carry out a more structured reflection on the impact any new strategies and approaches have had on your students. As with everything that happens in education, we are all on a constant journey of self-improvement and undoubtedly there will be further changes to your practice in the weeks and months ahead. However, it is important that you take some time now to judge the effectiveness of what you have been trialing before deciding whether to continue on the same path or stop and try something else.

How and why to complete the questionnaire

In order to compete the questionnaire, you will not only have to evaluate how effective your stretch and challenge provision is now you have trialed various strategies or approaches, but you will also need to speak to your students and colleagues. Remember that we do not work in isolation and it is crucial that we get useful, honest and constructive feedback from our colleagues and students. We might think that a particular strategy has made a significant difference but our students may tell us something we are not aware of; similarly, our colleagues might see something with a fresh pair of eyes and be able to suggest other ways of planning our stretch and challenge provision that we may not have considered.

If you feel that you are not in a position to complete the questionnaire yet, then it would be a good idea to go through the takeaways at the end of each chapter and commit to completing some parts of the 'To do' lists to enable you to move forward with your stretch and challenge provision.

You will remember the questionnaire process from chapter 3 (page 33), but here is a reminder.

Quick response approach

If your preference for the self-evaluation is to go with your gut only, then simply fill in the quick response section after each question with the first thing that comes into your mind when you ask yourself the question. Do not mull over the question too long, simply read carefully and answer quickly. This approach will give you an overview of your current stretch and challenge practice and will take relatively little time. Just make sure you are uninterrupted, in a quiet place and able to complete the questionnaire in one sitting with no distractions so that you get focused and honest answers.

Considered response approach

If you choose to take a more reflective and detailed approach, then you can leave the quick response section blank and go straight onto reading the further guidance section under each question. This guidance provides prompt questions and ideas to get you thinking in detail about the question being answered and is designed to open up a wider scope in your answer. It will also enable you to look at your experience and pull examples into your answer to back up your statements. You may want to complete it a few questions at a time and take breaks, or you may be prepared to simply sit and work through the questions all in one sitting to ensure you remain focused. This approach does take longer, but it can lead to a more in-depth understanding of your current stretch and challenge practice, and you will gain much more from the process than the quick response alone.

Combined approach

A thorough approach, and one I recommend, would be to use both approaches together regardless of personal preference. There is clear value in both approaches being used together. This would involve you firstly answering the self-evaluation quick response questions by briefly noting down your instinctual answers for all questions. The next step would be to return to the start of the self-evaluation, read

• I have done this self-assessment before. • I only want a surface level overview of my current understanding and practice. • I work better when I work at speed. • I don't have much time.	Quick
• I have never done this self-assessment before. • I want a deeper understanding of my current understanding and practice. • I work better when I take my time and really think things over. • I have some time to do this self-assessment.	Considered
• I have never done this self-assessment before. • I have done this self-assessment before. • I want a comprehensive and full understanding of my current understanding and practice and want to compare that to what I thought before taking the self-assessment. • I have a decent amount of time to dedicate to completing this self-assessment.	Combined

Fig. 21 How should I approach the self-evaluation questionnaire

the further guidance and then answer the questions once more, slowly and in detail forming more of a narrative around each question and pulling in examples from your own experience. Following this you would need to read over both responses and form a comprehensive and honest summary in your mind of your answers and a final view of where you feel you stand right now in your stretch and challenge practice.

This is the longest of the three approaches to this questionnaire but will give you a comprehensive and full understanding of your current stretch and challenge practice. You will be surprised at the difference you see between the quick response and the considered response answers to the same questions. It can be very illuminating.

Rating	Definition
1	Not at all. I don't. None at all. Not happy. Not confident at all.
2	Rarely. Barely. Very little. Very unconfident.
3	Not often at all. Not much. Quite unconfident.
4	Not particularly. Not really. Not a lot. Mildly unconfident.
5	Neutral. Unsure. Don't know. Indifferent.
6	Sometimes. At times. Moderately. A little bit. Mildly confident.
7	Quite often. A fair bit. Some. A little confident.
8	Most of the time. More often than not. Quite a lot. Quite confident.
9	The majority of the time. A lot. Very confident.
10	Completely. Very much so. A huge amount. Extremely happy. Extremely confident.

Fig. 22 Rate yourself definitions

Rate yourself

The final part of the self-evaluation is to rate yourself. This section will ask you to rate your confidence and happiness in each area that has been covered in the questionnaire, with a view to working on these areas for improvement throughout the course of the book. The table below shows how the scale works: the higher the number you allocate yourself, the better you feel you are performing in that area.

Stretch and challenge questionnaire

QUESTION 1: Which pedagogical approaches have you considered or tried that you have liked in terms of stretching your students?

Quick response:

_____

_____

_____

_____

Questions for consideration

- How have you tweaked your pedagogical approach to planning to ensure excellent progress for all learners?
- What new routines have you established in your lessons and how have they been received by the students?
- Which aspects of pedagogy that you have considered have had the most impact on your students?

Considered response:

_____

_____

_____

_____

_____

_____

_____

Rate yourself

QUESTION 1: How happy are you with the pedagogical approaches to stretch and challenge you have focused on so far?

| 1 | 2 | 3 | 4 | 5 | 6 | 7 | 8 | 9 | 10 |

QUESTION 2: What practical strategies do you feel have had an impact on students' attainment and achievement?

Quick response:

_____

_____

_____

_____

Questions for consideration

- Which strategies have resulted in positive learning gains for your students?
- Which strategies have you tried but then needed to tweak for your own student context?
- Were there any surprises that you hadn't considered before you implemented the new strategies?

Considered response:

_____

_____

_____

_____

_____

_____

_____

_____

_____

_____

_____

_____

Rate yourself

QUESTION 2: How much impact on attainment and achievement do you feel your chosen strategies have had for your students?

1   2   3   4   5   6   7   8   9   10

QUESTION 3: How has your understanding of stretch and challenge changed after engaging with the ideas in this book?

Quick response:

_____

_____

_____

_____

Questions for consideration

- How has your everyday approach to stretch and challenge changed?
- How has your approach to long-term planning changed?
- Have you used different types of hard and soft data to diagnose your students' barriers to learning?

Considered response:

_____

_____

_____

_____

_____

_____

_____

_____

_____

_____

_____

Rate yourself

QUESTION 3: How happy are you with your current practice with regards to stretching all of your students?

1   2   3   4   5   6   7   8   9   10

QUESTION 4: Which educational thinkers and research have you found most interesting and how has this influenced your practice?

Quick response:

_____

_____

_____

_____

Questions for consideration

- Which educational thinkers have you engaged with whilst reading this book?
- Which research are you keen to invest more time reading about as you continue to develop your practice?
- How are you going to make time to build in engaging with wider reading and research to support your development?

Considered response:

_____

_____

_____

_____

_____

_____

_____

_____

_____

_____

Rate yourself

QUESTION 4: How confident are you with your knowledge of educational research into what works to increase student challenge?

1	2	3	4	5	6	7	8	9	10

QUESTION 5: How have you identified, tried out and tweaked particular strategies to ensure they are appropriate for your age- and subject-specific context?

Quick response:

_____

_____

_____

_____

Questions for consideration

- Which pedagogical approaches to stretch and challenge need to be embedded into your department to increase student outcomes?
- Which specific strategies based upon educational research would have most impact on the learning in your subject?
- Is any part of what you have learnt about stretch and challenge in conflict with any policies and practices in your department?

Considered response:

_____

_____

_____

_____

_____

_____

_____

_____

_____

_____

Rate yourself

QUESTION 5: How confident are you in changes needed to subject-specific practices on a departmental level?

| 1 | 2 | 3 | 4 | 5 | 6 | 7 | 8 | 9 | 10 |

QUESTION 6: What have you shared or discussed with colleagues in your school about what you have learnt about stretch and challenge?

Quick response:

_____

_____

_____

_____

Questions for consideration

- How have you influenced practice in your department?
- Have you sought out opportunities to share and discuss ideas outside of your department?
- What could you do to disseminate your findings across the whole school and affect change?

Considered response:

_____

_____

_____

_____

_____

_____

_____

_____

_____

_____

Rate yourself

QUESTION 6: How confident are you about sharing your ideas with colleagues on a whole-school level?

| 1 | 2 | 3 | 4 | 5 | 6 | 7 | 8 | 9 | 10 |

QUESTION 7: Where do you feel you have made the most progress in your ability to challenge all students to work outside their comfort zone and accelerate their progress?

Quick response:

_____

_____

_____

_____

Questions for consideration

- What would you consider your strengths are with regards to stretch and challenge?
- Have these strengths changed since completing your initial self-evaluation?
- What positive feedback have you received from colleagues, students or parents since your initial self-evaluation?

Considered response:

_____

_____

_____

_____

_____

_____

_____

_____

_____

_____

Rate yourself

QUESTION 7: How happy are you with the changes you have made to become a more effective and reflective practitioner?

1   2   3   4   5   6   7   8   9   10

QUESTION 8: Where do you feel your weaknesses are with regards to stretch and challenge?

Quick response:

_____

_____

_____

_____

Questions for consideration

- What would you now consider are your areas for development?
- Have these areas for development changed since your initial self-evaluation?
- How exactly are you going to continue to develop and improve your current practice?

Considered response:

_____

_____

_____

_____

_____

_____

_____

_____

_____

_____

_____

_____

Rate yourself

QUESTION 8: How much do you feel you need to improve your areas of weakness in your stretch and challenge provision?

| 1 | 2 | 3 | 4 | 5 | 6 | 7 | 8 | 9 | 10 |

QUESTION 9: How have you interacted with your students when engaging with different approaches to stretch and challenge?

Quick response:

_____

_____

_____

_____

Questions for consideration

- Have you sought out your students' views of the different strategies you have implemented?
- How have you had to tweak your implementation of strategies based on feedback from your students?
- Is there anything that went particularly well with individuals or groups of students?

Considered response:

_____

_____

_____

_____

_____

_____

_____

_____

_____

Rate yourself

QUESTION 9: How confident are you that you are working with students to remove their barriers to learning and accelerating their progress?

| 1 | 2 | 3 | 4 | 5 | 6 | 7 | 8 | 9 | 10 |

QUESTION 10: How have you interacted with parents and carers in terms of your approach to stretching all of your students out of their comfort zone and developing them as learners?

Quick response:

_____

_____

_____

_____

Questions for consideration

- Have you discussed any new strategies that you have implemented with parents and carers?
- Have you invited parents and carers to give you feedback on any changes they have noticed?
- Have you asked parents and carers to talk with students about their learning and what you could do to support them further?

Considered response:

_____

_____

_____

_____

_____

_____

_____

_____

Rate yourself

QUESTION 10: How confident are you when it comes to involving parents and carers in discussions about how to stretch students and develop their learning?

1	2	3	4	5	6	7	8	9	10

QUESTION 11: What are your next steps to further develop your understanding and planning for stretch and challenge?

Quick response:

_____

_____

_____

_____

Questions for consideration

- Which changes are you going to continue to embed in your practice?
- What is the next thing you would want to trial in your approach to stretch and challenge?
- Which individual students or groups of students are you going to focus on next?

Considered response:

_____

_____

_____

_____

_____

_____

_____

_____

_____

_____

_____

Rate yourself

QUESTION 11: How happy are you with your plans to continue developing your practice?

1	2	3	4	5	6	7	8	9	10

The results

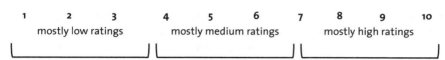

Fig. 23 How did you rate yourself?

Mostly low ratings

Although you have made a start in developing your stretch and challenge provision, you still need to spend time thinking more deeply about ensuring that all of your students are appropriately challenged in your classes. It would be a good idea to complete more of the activities on the 'To do' lists. In addition, you should get another colleague on board who can support you to develop your use of different approaches and strategies.

Mostly medium ratings

You have made some effective changes to your practice and your students are beginning to feel the impact of these changes. It is clear that you have engaged with research and other wider reading to ensure that the approaches you have taken are suitable for your own class context. Your next step is to identify the areas of the questionnaire where you scored lowest and make these the priority over the next few weeks and months so that you can continue to develop high-quality stretch and challenge opportunities in your classes which will lead to excellent student achievement.

Mostly high ratings

Your responses to the questionnaire indicate that you have a very clear sense of what it is you are trying to achieve with regards to how you stretch your students. After engaging in extensive reading and building excellent relationships with colleagues and students who are working with you to ensure maximum learning gains, now is the time to consider how you can begin to support others to become highly proficient. Have a look at the training plans in Part 2 of this book and reflect on what role you could take in delivering some of these possible CPD options.

Now what?

Now you have reflected on how far you have come, it is important to create a realistic plan of how you will keep developing your practice. We all know that feeling of returning from an INSET and promising ourselves we are going to do a whole heap of things to become better teachers; the reality is often a short-lived attempt to change practice. To make long-lasting changes, you need to decide on what will have the most impact on your students but also take into consideration how much effort you will need to invest to make the changes. Some strategies and approaches require a much greater effort on the teacher's part so you need to think carefully about how you will continue to embed these changes when you are run off your feet and are at critical stressful points in the school year. What may seem like a good idea in September doesn't always feel that way in March!

Once you have decided which strategies you are going to continue to use and with which students, your next step is to decide which new strategies you want to trial. Again, don't take on too much; it is much better to select one or two new strategies rather than go for a wholesale change to your existing practice. It is confusing for students and you are setting yourself up to fail. There are different ways of approaching which new strategies to trial; you could concentrate on a particular aspect of pedagogy such as questioning and make that the focus for all of your classes or you might decide to focus on individual students that you know aren't making good progress with their learning. Remember, whether you are focusing on specific individuals or specific aspects of pedagogy, don't forget to involve your students and their parents or carers so that everyone is clear what it is you are trying to achieve. Make explicit not just the 'what' but the 'why' so when students inevitably begin to struggle, they have a clear understanding as to why they are experiencing these changes.

Ultimately, stretch and challenge is all about knowing your students really, really well – but this takes time! Observe them, involve them, talk to them and use as many sources of evidence as possible to make informed judgements about what might make a positive difference on how they are developing as effective learners. However, it is a process of trial and error. What works for one student might not work for another with similar data; a strategy that worked really well with one class could fall flat with your new class. Always be alert and responsive to the needs of the students you have in front of you. Use this book as a guide but don't be afraid to tweak your practice to take into account your own school context.

Chapter 6 takeaway

Teaching tip

Keep going!

The first thing that can go out of the window when we are stuck in the daily grind of teaching is reflection time. Sometimes you feel like you've got so much to get through, it's easy to just rehash something you used last year and keep your fingers crossed that students will learn something. Yet it is so important to build in time for honest reflection. At the end of each week, think about the lessons you've taught and which ones you are happy with and which ones you'd rather forget. Why did this lesson go better than that one? Don't be too hard on yourself but do remain objective about your practice so that you don't plateau.

Pass it on

Sharing your ideas – blogging

As you have seen throughout this book, each chapter has ended with a recommendation of a blog to read to extend your thinking on stretch and challenge. The world of blogging has given teachers an excellent platform to share and discuss their views. It can be a different experience to reading an academic piece of research as often the blogs are practical and relatable, not to mention much shorter than academic papers. Despite it being really important to set aside time to engage with current academic research, it is not always easy to do so; consequently, you may want to build up a list of high-quality blogs and bookmark them so that you can dip in and out of them when you have a spare 15 minutes.

Not only should you engage with blogs but you too could become a blogger. At this point in the book, you will have carried out some interesting action research on your students by engaging in reading, selecting some strategies to try and reflecting on the success of these new approaches. Teachers are interested in reading about experiences from an authentic voice – think of it as an extended staffroom conversation. Two accessible platforms you could use to set up your blog are wordpress.com or blogger.com. If this seems like too much to commit to, then you could write short pieces and upload to staffrm.io, a platform for those who want to share their experiences but don't want to set up their own blog. Set yourself a challenge of contributing a short piece every half term, updating the community on your progress with developing your understanding of stretch and challenge.

Share with staff
By now, you will have amassed a lot of information from wider reading and your own work with your students. Think about how much you have learnt from committing to improving your practice – you are certainly modelling to your students what it means to do something out of your comfort zone and stretching yourself to always improve. Yet if all this great learning gets stuck in your classroom then you will have missed an opportunity for affecting change on a wider scale. Could you volunteer to present at your department meeting about what you've been doing? Or is there a teaching and learning platform at your school that you could use to share your experiences and get others excited about trying something new? We don't like to blow our own trumpets – we prefer to keep our heads down and get on with the job – but we are doing our school community a disservice if we have all of this good practice going on across the school but no joined-up thinking about how we can learn from each other.

Share and tweet
Share your progress so far and reflections on what you have learnt on Twitter using the hashtag #BloomsCPD.

CPD book club recommendation
John Hattie and Gregory Yates, *Visible Learning and the Science of How We Learn* (see Bibliography and further reading, page 272)

Bloggers' corner
Belmont Community School has set up a fantastic blog sharing teachers' experiences of trying new pedagogical approaches and teaching strategies with their students. It is a reflective blog and there are many ideas to read about to inspire you to keep developing your own practice. Visit the blog at belmontteach.wordpress.com.

TO DO LIST:

- ❏ Invite another school to carry out a learning walk around your school focusing on stretch and challenge
- ❏ Share what you have learnt about stretch and challenge at the next department meeting
- ❏ Share your journey to becoming a stretch and challenge expert using the hashtag #BloomsCPD
- ❏ Read Belmont School's blog about improving their whole-school stretch and challenge approach at belmontteach.wordpress.com
- ❏ Read *Visible Learning and the Science of How We Learn* by John Hattie and Gregory Yates

7

Embedding and developing the practice

Now you have considered your own practice over an extended period of time and experimented with new ways of working in your classroom, it is time to think about how you can create a long-term culture of development for you and your colleagues. What can you do to ensure that you continue to have impact in your own classroom as well as broaden your experiences to encourage other colleagues to come on board and make stretch and challenge their focus?

The question to start with is this: why put stretch and challenge at the centre of everything you do? There are other important things that you could focus on that would have impact – marking and feedback, use of digital technology or literacy to name a few. Nonetheless, I see stretch and challenge as a moral imperative. Everything begins and ends with stretch and challenge – again, don't confuse this concept with differentiation. Differentiation is reductionist; stretch and challenge is aspirational. Just imagine if every single student you came into contact with was working at optimum levels which pushed them out of their comfort zone and into the challenge zone. What would a classroom or a school look like where this was the norm? It is a very exciting notion but difficult to achieve. Why? You can't fake it. Unless you are committed to finding out about the needs and talents of all of your students, then you're not in a place where you can put stretch and challenge at the heart of all you do. So when colleagues ask you why they should be focusing on this at the expense of something else, encourage them to take the broader view of education as a means of giving students greater life opportunities now and later.

Below are suggestions for how you can continue your quest to improving your practice as well as inspiring others to come with you on this journey.

Create your vision for success

There's no way you will be in a position to encourage others to get involved if you do not have clarity of purpose and vision about what you want to achieve. Spend time creating your vision of the culture and climate you want in your classes.

- What are your expectations for every student you teach and how do you communicate this to them?
- How will students get involved in building this purposeful learning environment?
- What are your goals with each class in the first half term?
- How do you envisage building on this good start and pushing students forward throughout the year?

You will need to prioritise what you are going to do as you can't do everything. Keep the vision clear and concise.

Set your radar

Make the students you want to target high profile. Share this information with those around you to allow them to share ideas and advice with you. Look at each of your classes and identify which students in these classes are not making the most of their potential.

- Do you know why these students aren't flying?
- Are the students themselves able to articulate their barriers to learning?
- What have you read that can help you work out which strategies to implement?
- What would success look like if the strategies were to have a positive impact?

Once you've decided on your students, create pen portraits of them and stick them in your planner to keep these students in mind at all times.

Conduct your own action research

Start off by doing some wider reading; it may be some of the blogs or book recommendations in this book or something you've found through Twitter. Once you've decided on your approach, share with your class and your colleagues that you are going to carry out some action research. Action research is a great way to try and affect change in your class as it doesn't require too much of a time investment but it does require reflection and evaluating what you are trying to achieve. It is a methodical approach to making marginal learning gains in your own classroom setting.

- What have you read as a starting point?
- What are the student's or students' barriers to learning?
- How are you going to try and remove them?
- What checking points are you going to put in place to measure the impact of your new approach?
- What support could you draw on to help you with your action research?

It is not a problem if you are going to carry out action research by yourself but if you can involve a colleague to come and offer a fresh pair of eyes and ears, you will probably make faster progress than working alone. If you are working alone, consider using video to capture what is going on in your class as what you *think* is happening might be quite different to the reality!

Empower the team

If you really believe that the approach you are taking is having significant impact on your students then it is natural that you will want to disseminate this with colleagues in your team. This may be fairly easy if you're a middle or senior leader but don't underestimate the enthusiasm of those newer to the profession – everyone appreciates a teacher trying to do their best for their students, however long or short you've been in the role.

- What would be the best way for you to share your journey so far?
- Do you have a range of data you can use as evidence to persuade colleagues that what you're doing is worth trying?
- Are you confident in sharing the highs and lows you've experienced and what you've learnt from failure as well as successes?
- Are you clear about what you would like your colleagues to do and how to get them on board to make a change?

Even if you just get one other colleague on board to trial things with you, that's potentially a hundred more students who you are having an impact on.

Set up a resource bank

We know that teachers love a good resource but resources take time to make and are the first things to fall by the wayside when teachers are under pressure. Yet a well-resourced lesson gives students a good chance of accessing the learning. Encourage colleagues to contribute to a school resource bank for stretch and challenge. Create categories based on the different approaches outlined in chapter 3 (page 33) or the ideas of the key educational thinkers in chapter 4 (page 57).

- What is the best way to lay out the resource bank?
- What platform is the best to use to share resources electronically?
- What resources would be useful for different types of students?
- Can the resource be easily tweaked for different subjects to use?

Without doubt, having a plethora of high-quality resources that teachers can access across school will improve the quality of teaching and learning.

Engage with research

You don't have to have been working in schools for long before you realise how little time is given to embedding key ideas. One year the focus might be AfL; then the next it could be marking; the year after it could be digital technology. Often it can feel like we're on a non-stop roundabout of initiatives with no pause for reflection. One way to stop this quest for the silver bullet and the onslaught of fads and gimmicks is to thoroughly engage with research and then spread the message across school as to what is proven to have significant impact.

- What high quality research are you engaging with?
- Has it been in a research review, as this is the gold standard?
- How might the research fit with your school context?
- Is there scope to get involved with your own in-school research or to apply to external organisations such as the Education Endowment Foundation (EEF)?
- How can the research be packaged and shared across the school so all teachers can access it quickly and digest the findings?

Becoming research-informed is at the heart of becoming an excellent teacher and ensuring you and your colleagues have the best chance of improving student outcomes.

Chapter 7 takeaway

Teaching tip
Always expect the best from students
Make sure your expectations of your students remain high. It is easy to fall into the trap of labelling students in different ways and forgetting that they are all individuals with particular needs and talents. As long as you are confident that you have got enough support and challenge in place, set the bar high and watch your students flourish. They will constantly surprise you!

Pass it on
Sharing your ideas – Edmodo
Edmodo is a fantastic platform to sign up to where you can share ideas with educational professionals across the world. It has the look and feel of Facebook and is extremely easy to navigate. You will be sent alerts and notifications via email once you've signed up so you can log on and read what others are saying about topics that are of interest to you. Join for free at www.edmodo.com.

Team discussion
As a team, it's important you scrutinise your data. Who is and isn't making progress? Are there any patterns? Don't work in silos. Be honest about who is struggling in your classes and sit down as a team to collate all of the wisdom in the room. Focus the discussion on ways of removing particular students' barriers to learning and ensure that you return to these students in a follow-up meeting to check if what you're trying is having impact.

Share and tweet
Share your experiences of how you are working with others to increase levels of challenge using the hashtag #BloomsCPD on Twitter.

CPD book club recommendation
Doug Lemov, Erica Woolway and Katie Yezzi, *Practice Perfect (see Bibliography and further reading, <XREF>)*

Bloggers' corner
Check out Nancy Gedge's blog, 'The Diary of a Not So Ordinary Boy' for inspiring posts on working with students with special educational needs. Visit notsoordinarydiary.wordpress.com.

TO DO LIST:

- ❑ Sign up to Edmodo so you can follow other teachers from around the world talking about stretch and challenge
- ❑ Work with your colleagues to analyse data and identify your students' barriers to learning
- ❑ Share your experiences of increasing the level of challenge in your classroom using the hashtag #BloomsCPD
- ❑ Check out Nancy Gedge's blog at notsoordinarydiary.wordpress.com
- ❑ Read *Practice Perfect* by Doug Lemov, Erica Woolway and Katie Yezzi

Part 2

Train others

1 Planning and preparing for your training

Before sharing with you a range of training plans to enable the delivery of in-house CPD on stretch and challenge, we need to consider why it is a good idea to move towards an in-house approach at the expense of external CPD. As well as this, this chapter looks at the role of the CPD lead and explores how to create the most effective CPD provision for staff. Finally, the chapter ends with some of my top tips for running in-house CPD.

Why you should do-it-yourself CPD!

If you had asked teachers a few years back what CPD they had done that year, you might expect them to discuss a course they had been on run by one of the main CPD course providers. If they were lucky enough to work at a school with a healthy budget, they may have gone on a couple of such courses that year. However, if you asked teachers in the current climate to discuss their CPD for the year, many may not have gone out onto any courses; instead, their school may cover CPD in-house and prioritise external courses that are run by exam boards so teachers can get the necessary information to plan their exam schemes of work.

It is not just a case of saving money – although there are few schools that are able to spend the same amount of money on external courses as they once did. The real benefits come from the opportunities to involve as many staff as possible in working towards a common school improvement goal. The benefit of in-house CPD, particularly when it is focused on stretch and challenge, is that those delivering and participating in the training are well aware of the specific school context. Often, it is much more effective to carry out CPD where the people in the room with you know the issues that the school faces on a daily basis. The CPD lead and those delivering training will be aware of particular students, the school's development plan and the needs of individual teachers.

Another important aspect of in-house CPD is that the CPD lead can create a package that focuses on short-term wins as well as longer-term goals. Progression, reflection and evaluation of impact on student outcomes should all be built into the training that is being delivered. The Teacher Development Trusts' report, *Developing Great Teaching*, makes some specific recommendations as to what schools need to do to create high-quality CPD for teachers. The key finding from the report was that the most effective professional development lasted at least two terms. When planning your in-house CPD, make sure that teachers are engaging with the same CPD focus for at least two terms; otherwise, the impact will be significantly limited. Moreover, the report states that a shared sense of purpose during professional development is an important factor for success. By teachers working together in school to support each other's CPD and raising the achievement of their own students, more can be achieved than in any one-off course.

Finally, deciding to run your own in-house CPD gives ample opportunity for members of staff to gain a sense of autonomy over their practice as well as develop key leadership capacity. Delivering in-house CPD means schools need to be talent spotting at all times to identify who is able to train other members of staff effectively. We need to empower our teachers to see that they are agents of change and that they have the ability to develop themselves. Ultimately, this model of CPD is about active participation where teachers take responsibility for their own development of knowledge and skills.

A note of caution though at this stage: be careful about relying on the same group of teachers all the time without taking into consideration their needs. Although it is important to talent spot and grow your leadership capacity, it is too easy to forget that everyone needs developing. If the same members of staff are always delivering the training, when are their opportunities to improve themselves? Some senior leaders may say that delivering training to staff is a CPD opportunity in itself and, of course, there is truth in this statement. Yet, no one is perfect and leaders of CPD need to be acknowledged, celebrated and offered other forms of CPD. For example, the Schools, Students and Teachers network (SSAT) offer qualifications for teachers to become lead practitioners. An alternative may be investing money to work with the organisation Teaching Leaders, who run well-established programmes in developing middle leaders.

External CPD courses

Despite all of the reasons above why it is incredibly effective to run in-house CPD, there are some points to consider about why certain external courses and external input may be warranted. Some external courses and conferences give teachers the opportunity to listen to expert educational professionals and gain high-quality advice and guidance. If the course fits with school development priorities then it may be worth investing money into a member of staff attending. Yet it needs to be made clear that whatever is taken away from the course needs to be disseminated to other teachers in school. There must be an expectation that the teacher is going to have to do something with the new knowledge they have gained from going on a particular course – and that has to be more than altering their own classroom practice. They need to share widely what they have heard and commit to supporting other colleagues to change their practice.

Another useful aspect of external courses is the ability to network with teachers from other schools who are also attending the same course. Going off-site for the day to attend a course isn't just about listening to the expert speakers; it is also about making the most of breaks and reflection time to talk to other teachers and see what they're doing in their schools. An expectation should be in place from leaders that talking to other professionals and making contacts is equally as important as sitting listening to one of the guest speakers.

Top tip

There are some fantastic organisations that support schools in offering advice, resources and networking opportunities. I've already mentioned the work of SSAT and Teaching Leaders, but I'd also highly recommend joining the Teacher Development Trust (TDT), formerly known as the National Teacher Enquiry Network (NTEN). The TDT offers a range of services to schools including a CPD audit against a set of robust criteria. Schools can see whether they are working at bronze, silver or gold level. After the audit, schools can decide which CPD model would work best for them and the TDT has a plethora of resources and an extensive research library to help CPD leads plan effective training. There are also research papers that focus on all of the stretch and challenge approaches discussed in Part 1, chapter 3 (page 33). Linked to this, there are many academic papers from the key educational thinkers in chapter 4 (page 57); this may be a useful way forward for some staff at your school who might want to read more about specific strategies to develop stretch and challenge in their class but do not have the time to read a whole book. Once you join the TDT, you will be connected to other schools and it is easy to make contact with a fellow TDT school and work together based on the needs of the school. Creating high-quality in-house CPD opportunities are only enhanced by the input of external organisations and the TDT report, *Developing Great Teaching*, mentioned on page 140) states that external facilitation is a common factor in successful outcomes, working sometimes in tandem with internal specialists. However, external input must offer support in a constructive, effective way.

Why you should do stretch and challenge DIY CPD

As I've said previously (page 126), good stretch and challenge is about knowing your students really, really well and in-house CPD is the most effective way of putting your own school context at the heart of training. You can't do stretch and challenge without considering the needs of your students and it is nigh impossible for an external speaker to tailor their training to cover all of the students in your class. But you know your students; and your colleagues sitting next to you in the staffroom know their students. Consequently, you've already got a head start on selecting CPD opportunities that will benefit your learners. Any CPD that takes place needs to focus on raising student achievement. This is a vital point that is often missed. Many CPD opportunities focus on developing outstanding teachers (with a nod to Ofsted) but the focus needs to be on the impact the training will have on student outcomes.

Furthermore, keeping the focus on your own students and how to stretch them should develop excellent relationships between teachers and students. If you ask students about their best teachers, what will crop up time and time again is that they pick teachers who they believe care about them and want them to do well (don't confuse this with the teacher being friends with their students!). If your students know that you are working on a particular approach that you hope will have a positive impact on their own achievement, then they will appreciate the effort that you are putting into them.

When managed and undertaken properly, running your own in-house CPD is incredibly satisfying. In your school, every teacher will have a certain area of expertise – from the NQT to the teacher with 20 years of experience. How rewarding to make use of the talents of the school instead of expecting an outsider to provide the silver bullet to radically improve student outcomes. For anyone who has ever trained colleagues, it can be a daunting prospect at first – we teachers have been known to be a tad cynical at being told what to do by a so-called expert . . . But the mood changes when you look up and see it is one of your own – someone you know teaches the same students as you do and who wants the best for them. They are not claiming to be an expert; rather, they are opening themselves up in an honest and reflective way to share their knowledge and work with other colleagues to bring about change.

How to choose the right teachers to lead your stretch and challenge CPD

If you are given the task of selecting teachers to run different parts of your CPD programme, it is important to select the right people. But who are the 'right' people? The ones with the best exam data? The ones who went on a good course? The ones who get good feedback in lesson observations? Perhaps. Yet, in the same way that not all highly-academic people make great teachers, just because someone is a great teacher doesn't necessarily qualify them to be a great facilitator of CPD. Great CPD facilitators have to have a real passion for learning and inspiring others: essentially, they have great leadership skills.

Here are some points to consider:

- Research tells us that the best CPD has subject-specific pedagogy at the heart of it. Therefore, it would be a good idea to try and create a group of 'lead learners' in your school, one in each department. You may be the overall CPD lead but you are not an expert in each subject area so see your role as supporting the work of those in each department who want to develop their colleagues and improve student achievement.
- Look at as much data as possible to identify the strengths of your potential lead learners. What are their strengths and how do you know? Try and triangulate your findings by drawing upon observations, student interviews, parental feedback, student progress data, previous areas of pedagogical interest and their willingness to develop themselves. The data should help you identify how different lead learners favour a particular approach to stretch and challenge. You could match different lead learners to different approaches from Part 1, chapter 3 (page 33).
- Once you have decided who you want as your lead learners, make sure they actually have the capacity to do whatever it is they are being asked to do. They may potentially be the most effective facilitators in school but if they have no time to plan and reflect on their sessions, then that potential will go to waste. Negotiations need to be made with the headteacher to ensure these people are given as much time as possible to work with each other to ensure consistency of standards in the training they are running. You cannot expect lead learners to speak confidently about the research of key educational thinkers from chapter 4 (page 57) if they are not given adequate time to read their work in full and reflect on how the research could be implemented by teachers to improve their students' academic achievement.

Choosing the right staff to deliver appropriate training and supporting them to feel confident in inspiring others gives a school the greatest chance of creating an effective learning culture.

Top tips

- **Seek out your NQTs** – when considering who might be the best people to support others with their CPD, NQTs are often overlooked because we think they are too inexperienced or need to practise their craft before helping others. Whilst this is true, an important way in which we can make use of our NQTs is to speak with them about their training. Teacher training constantly evolves and what they have just been learning about may be new to more experienced members of staff. Especially now that PGCE courses can lead to a Masters accreditation, new teachers are expected to engage with current research in a more systematic way than ever before. New members of staff need to share this research with their colleagues. NQTs may feel uncomfortable doing this so create a format in which this can occur regularly. Perhaps you could create a 'NQT research corner' in the staff teaching and learning bulletin.
- **Replace traditional departmental meetings with CPD forums** – often departmental meetings can get bogged down in administrative tasks and information sharing that could have been done via email. Alternate traditional departmental meetings with departmental CPD forums in which the team get together to discuss a particular approach to stretch and challenge or some of the strategies mentioned in chapter 4 (page 57). A department might want to make homework their focus for stretching students' learning outside of class; or in larger departments, each teacher might focus on one of the key educational thinkers mentioned in chapter 4 (page 57) and share what they have learnt with their colleagues in departmental CPD forums. Rotate the chair for these meetings to give all of the team a chance to select the focus. Not only is this a great way for colleagues to reflect on their practice but it is also a means of creating a departmental identity and establishing a set of expectations about learning in your subject area.

Supporting other teachers

Putting together a comprehensive CPD programme for a school is a complex business: you need to get into the same mindset as you would if you were planning a scheme of work for a mixed-ability class! The staff is not a homogenous group and you need to take into consideration the strengths and weaknesses of every teacher and their confidence levels when it comes to planning high-quality stretch and challenge provision. At the same time, you need to balance individual staff needs with working towards a common goal of implementing your school development plan and its focus on stretch and challenge. A teacher may want to develop their use of digital technology but they would need to be encouraged to think how that fits into the wider school stretch and challenge plan of improving outcomes of students. A focus on digital technology may be useful if it was part of a larger focus on the use of resources to challenge our students further. Or, the teacher might want to develop feedback practices using digital technology and track how students are closing their learning gaps. The best schools have a shared sense of purpose and vision and the CPD programme needs to underpin that at all times to ensure cohesion.

The CPD journey in my school has been a long one! We had quite a traditional approach to CPD with INSET in the hall and a few after-school twilight sessions. Then, for a number of years, we had the whole school engaging in coaching and 'Lesson study' (see below) as the preferred CPD provision. Recently, we've begun to personalise our CPD offer based on the needs of departments. The more we've researched into effective CPD, the more we've discovered the need for staff to engage in subject-specific CPD as well as general aspects of pedagogy, so we have brought that focus into all of our options. Each head of subject discusses with their SLT line manager which CPD option would be most useful for members of their team: regular coaching focusing on identified students, trios working on lesson study or collaborative work on developing a challenging curriculum.

Linked to this is more effective use of appraisal. Each member of staff has a CPD target for their appraisal alongside another target based on the DfE *Teachers' Standards*. If the member of staff holds a Teaching and Learning Responsibility (TLR), then there is a third target based on leading their team. Having appraisal linked closely to the CPD programme highlights to staff how seriously the school takes professional development. This change to appraisal has had a significant impact on teachers' attitudes to professional development; CPD is not just for new or struggling staff. CPD is an entitlement for every member of staff because everyone can improve if given the time.

Coaching

Coaching is not to be confused with mentoring. Mentoring is hierarchical with the assumption that one person has a certain body of knowledge to pass onto a colleague. Coaching is not about providing the answers but helping a colleague find their own solutions by posing the right questions. Coaching is not easy, and those teachers selected to be coaches need to be trained effectively. It is worth spending money on a group of teachers going on a coaching course, as it is easy to slip into mentoring mode if you do not fully understand the coaching principles. Organisations such as Teaching Leaders provide coaching training as part of their programme, so if you have anyone who has completed an external qualification, they may be able to coach others to become coaches. Not only can coaching be used to develop teaching practice, it can also be used to develop leadership skills.

However, coaching lives and dies by the pairing so it is crucial to get the right people talking to each other. It actually takes a long time to get the pairings right. For example, if the two members of the pair are close friends, will they be able to approach the relationship in a detached, professional manner? Or, if the coach is a relatively inexperienced member of school but is coaching a teacher who is known to be disengaged with CPD, will they have the ability to help that teacher see things differently? There are no rights and wrongs with deciding on pairings – speak to as many people as possible to get their views and then approach the potential coach to see how they feel about coaching a particular member of staff. Make clear why you have selected this possible pairing as there may be other agendas that you are not aware of! Many schools are now using coaching as part of their core CPD offer and are reaping the benefits of this approach to teacher development.

Stretch and challenge is a particularly fruitful area for coaching as it allows teachers to focus on individual students. Quality coaching conversations will help teachers to move away from looking at a more general picture of their class and drill down into identifying how specific students are responding to the teacher's stretch and challenge strategies.

Lesson study

Returning to the TDT report *Developing Great Teachers* (page 142), there are a number of recommendations they make for securing effective, impactful CPD provision. One of the recommendations is to develop the use of peer learning but to also acknowledge that collaboration needs to be highly structured and managed. The report states that peer support and learning is a fundamental ingredient of effective professional development but it is not sufficient in its own right. Providers and schools should allow participants to engage in collegial problem-solving approaches that are focused on improving student outcomes.

Lesson study is one way of ensuring that collaborative learning has a positive impact on student outcomes. Lesson study is not about looking for quick wins – although there will most likely be some easy tweaks to practise that result in improved student achievement. This is not the aim of lesson study; the premise of lesson study is to:

- invest time in engaging with current research
- construct an enquiry question about a group of students
- engage in joint planning
- observe each other to see if planned strategies have any impact on learning
- reflect on the lessons as a group
- tweak practice and engage in further joint planning
- repeat the process over an extended period of time.

Lesson study is extremely beneficial for teachers and students as it is an enquiry-based model; it encourages teachers to experiment with current research and put it into the context of their own classes. It is a reflective process with the focus firmly positioned on students. Observations do not focus on the teacher but on the reaction of the students. No judgement is being made about the effectiveness of the teacher but on the usefulness of the teaching approach for that particular group of students. Finally it gives a small window of insight into the world of research and for those members of staff who really engage with the process, there could be the opportunity to get more members of staff to trial their findings with new classes the following year and affect change on a wider level.

As I've said before, stretch and challenge is about knowing your students really well and lesson study ties in nicely with this as the focus is on observing students learning in class as opposed to watching the teacher and judging their performance. The enquiry questions used as part of lesson study can be easily tailored so that teachers can narrow down their enquiry question to a particular approach from Part 1, chapter 3 (page 33) or a specific use of a strategy from chapter 4 (page 57).

Curriculum scrutiny

It doesn't matter how brilliant a teacher might be, if the curriculum is lacking, student progress will be limited. As teachers, we can get bogged down in the day-to-day planning of lessons, but individual lessons aren't as important as the schemes of work that make up that subject curriculum. The best schemes of work have stretch and challenge at the heart of them. Teachers could focus their attentions on evaluating the learning intentions for the scheme of work, the resources that have been created, the homework planned to extend the learning or the opportunities for teachers and students to participate in high-quality questioning and discussion.

An excellent form of CPD for teachers is to engage with other members of their team and scrutinise their subject curriculum. In a similar way to lesson study, it is an enquiry-based model of CPD; teachers consider how the curriculum meets the needs of a particular group of students, e.g. high-achieving students on entry, or students with low levels of literacy. The group of teachers challenge each other to see how the current schemes of work can be tweaked to ensure greater student progress based on wider reading and research. Different competing models of curriculum planning are considered and teachers experiment with teaching the same topic but refining the pedagogical approach and resources used to teach the students. Teachers in the group meet regularly to discuss how their classes have reacted to the new schemes of work. Coupled with this, teachers analyse students' progress data to see the impact of the new scheme of work and identify whether students' progress is being accelerated. As part of the curriculum scrutiny process, the team present their rationale, research and changes to curriculum to other colleagues and get feedback on possible improvements. Student voice is central to curriculum planning as student feedback is recorded at the start, middle and end of each scheme of work.

At the end of the year, each team working on curriculum scrutiny presents the key findings to other teams working on similar projects. If the new approach to curriculum planning proves successful, other departments take on board some of the principles and see if they have the same effect in their own subject area.

Top tip

Build a culture of sharing

All three of the approaches discussed above are collegiate in nature; no one is claiming to have the magic silver bullet, but what they all have in common is the desire to try new things and learn from others. Spread the culture of sharing by being an active voice in the staffroom; be a 'radiator' as opposed to a 'drain' and play your part in developing an exciting culture of learning amongst staff.

CPD book club recommendation

Dylan Wiliam, *Embedded Formative Assessment*. (See Bibliography and further reading, page 273) This is a great read, combining high-quality research with practical strategies to implement with your classes. If you are interested in developing your use of learning intentions, setting up groupings for effective collaboration or improving your use of feedback to support students in closing their learning gaps, then this book will help you refine your practice in these areas.

Bloggers' corner

Harry Fletcher-Wood has a keen interest in all things CPD and self-improvement. On his blog, there are multiple posts about his trials of specific questioning strategies to stretch his students. Check out his blog at improvingteaching.co.uk.

Joe Kirby is also very keen on developing more structured and research-led approaches to changing practice. There are some insightful posts on how he has engaged with the work of Daniel Willingham to challenge his students and develop their long-term memories. Check out his blog at pragmaticreform.wordpress.com.

Working with other schools

In this rapidly changing educational landscape where more and more schools are joining with others to form alliances and multi-academy trusts, it is seen as beneficial for schools to work with each other to improve student outcomes. In reality, genuine collaboration can be difficult to organise as each school has its own issues and agendas. Nonetheless, when schools do find a way of carrying out genuine collaboration, then it is a very useful process as schools can identify best practice, share it widely, work together to solve problems and develop a range of teachers, all of which will have a knock-on effect on student outcomes. The role of the local authority (LA) in helping schools to network is dwindling and it is now up to headteachers, the senior leadership team (SLT) and other middle leaders to try and establish useful links with other schools. Even in the best workplaces, staff can plateau and become blinkered if the school is not outward-looking. A fresh pair of eyes or a new perspective can rejuvenate staff and make them reconsider what they believe is the best way forward for improving their practice.

The specific form of the CPD between schools will depend on the needs of individual teachers or the school as a whole. Two schools might decide that a particular group of students in their schools is underachieving, e.g. Year 7 students with low levels of literacy, as mentioned in one of the case studies in chapter 5 (page 83). Or two schools might want to join up if they have a specific department that is working on a particular stretch and challenge approach. Two maths departments might both be working on building up a resource bank to stretch their high-achieving students, for example. If you have a role to play in encouraging collaboration between schools, you should think about:

- Choosing who will represent your school – will they be able to articulate the values and aims of the school?
- Identifying school priorities – how will the collaboration mutually benefit both schools, in terms of staff development and student achievement?
- Spreading the knowledge – how will the collaboration between schools get shared across a range of people not directly involved?
- Planning for the future – what possibilities are there for this particular collaboration to extend into other opportunities if this initial collaboration is a success?

For collaboration between schools to stand the best chance of a successful outcome, you will need to define well in advance the goals of all participating. Once these have been established and aligned, the participants will need to commit to a set of actions with clear deadlines. Regular time will need to be built in (this could be in person, via email or a Skype conversation) to review the collaborative work and evaluate the impact of the work carried out.

Below are a few ways in which you could set up effective partnerships with other schools.

TeachMeets

If there is no prior history of working with a particular school, an easy and informal way of establishing links could be to set up a TeachMeet. At a TeachMeet, people are invited to talk for either three minutes or seven minutes on a topic linked to the overall theme. If another school was interested in working on stretch and challenge, then this would be a great way of sharing best practice. Having the two different time slots encourages more people to take part and speak to their colleagues. A three-minute presentation might be sharing a particular strategy they've trialled with a class; a seven-minute presentation might be a more detailed sharing of a lesson study project. Presentations are grouped together to allow questions after each cluster of presentations to encourage audience engagement and participation in the TeachMeet.

When inviting other schools to the TeachMeet, decide in advance the subcategories for presentations to ensure there is not too much repetition and to keep the audience interested. For a stretch and challenge TeachMeet, you might have the following categories:

- Getting students out of their comfort zone
- Improving long-term memory

- Encouraging greater independence through student choice
- Improving questioning and discussion
- Developing students' literacy
- Creating a purposeful learning environment
- Developing a growth mindset
- Deploying TAs effectively
- Constructing and sharing learning outcomes
- Designing challenging homework
- Scaffolding learning to enable greater levels of challenge
- Learning collaboratively.

Don't forget to set up a hashtag for the TeachMeet and encourage others to tweet about what they are learning with the wider educational community.

Support and challenge buddies

This form of CPD works best with two members of staff who are operating at a similar level who can support each other with subject-specific issues they may be facing but also challenge each other to develop their knowledge and understanding. In particular, heads of department can benefit hugely from seeing another head of department in their subject area in a different school. Heads of department can team up within school too, but there is a danger that heads of department in the same school can suffer from 'we've always done it that way' syndrome. Seeing someone else do your role in a different way can be an illuminating experience; it can help you to reflect on your current practice and consider new ways of working and developing staff and students. For example, two members of staff might be teaching a class for which they have a TA working alongside them. The teachers agree to create checklists for their TAs to use so they can support a particular group of students in the class. The teachers then meet and share their resources and reflect on what impact they had on the students' progress.

In a similar way to coaching, the success of the buddy system relies on a relationship built on trust and openness. If SLT just decide to bring two people together without setting out a clear rationale or identifying why the partnering would be mutually beneficial, then it is likely to be tokenistic collaboration. Careful consideration needs to be given to the strengths of each teacher and how they can support each other. Once trust has been established, pairing up with someone outside of your school can actually lead to franker conversations as the other person won't have their own agenda they're pushing or be worried that what they say will get back to their line manager.

Cross-school assessment moderation

Another effective means of collaboration is to invite members of staff from different schools to come together to mark pieces of work together and moderate their judgements. This is quite time-intensive and most likely won't happen more than once a term; even once a term would indeed have great impact on marking procedures in a team. What can happen in schools is that a department gets used to working with each other and gets used to certain types of students they come into contact with every day. As a result, less thought goes into how a piece of work is meeting the marking criteria and gut instinct is employed. When teachers have to justify to a colleague from another school about how they have arrived at a particular mark, it forces them to really think deeply about how they are assessing students and the feedback they are offering to challenge the student further.

Alternatively, moderation can be used to discuss the quality of assessments a department is using in a particular scheme of work. If schools are teaching the same topic, it can be fascinating to see the different modes of assessment used to diagnose how much a student has learned. One department may only be using extended writing to assess students whereas another department might be experimenting with multiple choice questions. A lot can be learnt by sharing with each other and being open to trialling new approaches. Another school with a fresh pair of eyes may be able to see how to tweak a particular assessment to make it more challenging or to make it more accessible to a particular group of students.

Feedback and marking practices are a crucial part of effective stretch and challenge as you can only know your students really well if you are planning opportunities to test what they know and can do and adapting future learning to take into consideration what you have learnt about them.

Transition planning

A really effective form of collaboration is when cross phases work together to evaluate the progression from one key stage to another. The transition from primary to secondary is well-documented and students' 'learning dip' is something all secondary teachers experience. What isn't documented as much is that secondary school teachers often underestimate what students can do in Year 6 and often repeat work students have already encountered – a sure-fire way of reducing challenge. How might a Year 7 scheme of work be more of a challenge than a Year 6 one? When students move into key stage four, what role do the key stage coordinators play in ensuring effective transition? Is the work at the end of key stage three suitably challenging so students are GCSE ready? Students can often excel at GCSE and then struggle at the start of key stage five; their ability to carry out wider reading and manage their own time can be a shock for many students. How can effective transition planning ensure that students are equipped to start further education?

Engaging in joint planning to ensure smoother transition can really boost student outcomes for a number of reasons. First, the level of challenge can be increased as teachers get a better understanding of what students have tackled in the previous key stage. Secondly, experts in each key stage are on hand to share the common barriers for learning and suggest how to remove them for students entering a new key stage. Thirdly, a more joined-up approach to curriculum planning means there should be a much clearer and coherent thought process involved than might be the case with stand-alone schemes of work.

We know planning challenging, well-resourced schemes of work takes a long time so working in partnership with other schools can reduce this burden and enable teachers to learn from each other's best practice.

CPD book club recommendation

Gordon Stobart, *The Expert Learner* (see Bibliography and further reading). Read this book to find out how people move from novice to expert in their chosen field. In his book, there are also many links to other books and academic research for you to read. Stobart's book is a good companion piece to Doug Lemov's *Practice Perfect* (see Bibliography and further reading), where a lot of the book focuses on mastery and becoming an expert.

Bloggers' corner

Chris Chivers writes eloquently about his experiences of inclusion in schools and what this means for teachers in their day-to-day practice. His blog offers practical strategies for planning to meet the needs of all learners. Check out his blog at chrischiversthinks.weebly.com/blog-thinking-aloud.

The CPD leader

The role of CPD leader is one of the most important roles in a school; to be able to perform the role successfully, the member of staff needs to have a wealth of knowledge to make informed decisions including the strengths and needs of every member of staff. In order to know this information, the CPD leader needs to work with staff to balance individual staff needs and the wider school development plan with its focus on stretch and challenge. Excellent communication skills are imperative in this role as is the ability to bring others with you; just because you are CPD leader doesn't mean you can run it all. In order to fulfil the role, it is absolutely vital that the headteacher supports the CPD leader by giving them enough time to do the job effectively. Without doubt, the best schools are those that have a comprehensive and well-run CPD programme and this cannot be done unless there is a highly competent member of staff coordinating CPD opportunities.

The budget

The CPD leader should have a substantial budget to work with if the headteacher is serious about improving teacher quality and raising student achievement. Considering students sit in front of teachers for many hours a week, it makes sense to prioritise spending money on developing teachers. The CPD leader is responsible for deciding on all aspects of CPD – in-house and external providers.

One challenge the CPD leader can face is members of staff wanting to go on expensive courses as the CPD leader has to judge what impact this will have on the individual, their students and other colleagues. The CPD leader has to weigh up whether they think the requested course can offer something different and more useful than what could be provided in-house or working in collaboration with other schools. Some staff may feel hard done by if their course is rejected but the message needs to go out to all staff at the start of every year that external courses need to deliver greater impact than what could be achieved by the CPD offer in school.

Another issue the CPD leader has to take into consideration is how to organise the CPD programme for the whole year. Everything costs money – including teacher time with regards to cover. If the CPD leader is asking lead learners to run stretch and challenge sessions, then the lead learners will need time off to plan the sessions. If the CPD leader sees coaching or lesson study at the heart of the programme, then time will be needed for staff to watch each other and meet afterwards to discuss and reflect. Likewise, if curriculum scrutiny is a CPD option, then members of staff working in teams to research curriculum design and refine current schemes of work will need time to meet and collaborate. An effective CPD leader will plan specific time slots for all of these opportunities to go ahead but that requires a logical and strategic thinker. Fitting all of this into the already jam-packed school calendar takes a lot of perseverance and negotiation! At our school, the CPD leader hands over a portion of the CPD budget to the cover budget at the start of the academic year to allow for cover supervisors to be used when CPD is taking place in school time.

External providers

If the CPD leader decides that they want to spend some of their budget on working with external providers, then they need to make sure they use their money wisely and do their homework. They may decide to pool their money with a neighbouring school to secure the services of a high-profile speaker. A note of caution here: yes, a key note speaker at an INSET day can be inspirational and set the tone for the rest of the day but unless the key note speaker offers more than just a speech – such as workshops or one-to-one consultations with key members of staff – then the impact of that speaker is minimal. Also be wary of external speakers who actually want to sell you something but package it up as a speech. The CPD leader needs to make sure that whomever they book, they have got positive reviews from colleagues at other schools or from people they follow on Twitter. A far less expensive option could be to use some of the videos of the key educational thinkers from chapter 4 (page 57) in which they share their ideas about how to develop high-quality stretch and challenge.

Another way of making the most of external providers may be to send a team from school to an all-day conference where there are multiple sessions running at the same time. If the conference has a good reputation, such as the Schools, Students and Teachers' Network (SSAT) national conference or the Festival of Education, then sending a team who have planned which sessions they want to see in advance could be financially advantageous as often there are discounts given for groups. As long as the sessions focus on the stretch and challenge approaches in chapter 3 (page 33) or on the ideas of the key educational thinkers in chapter 4 (page 57) and the members of staff are committed to not only disseminating ideas but acting upon them, then you could argue that it is value for money.

CPD tracking

At the end of each academic year, it is advisable that you conduct a staff CPD audit to identify future CPD needs and tie these to the whole-school stretch and challenge plan. This can be done using a paper system but I would advise that you move to a paperless system as it's all too easy for bits of paper to go missing. Many companies, such as BlueSky which we use, offer software that will tailor a programme towards the needs of your school but it will enable the CPD leader to link CPD opportunities to areas of development identified through the CPD audit. The CPD leader can decide to give access to this information to appraisers and senior leaders. Uploading all of the CPD that the member of staff has carried out creates an online portfolio that gives a real sense of satisfaction.

Celebrating staff achievement

An important aspect of the CPD leader's role is to highlight members of staff who are putting in extra effort to develop their stretch and challenge practice and give their students the best chance of experiencing success. The CPD leader should have a regular slot at SLT meetings and staff briefings to highlight individuals who are making progress through CPD. Not only does this motivate members of staff to continue putting in extra effort but it also inspires others to experiment with their practice. The CPD leader should also ensure they don't forget to celebrate the rest of the CPD team who support the delivery of stretch and challenge training sessions. At our school, we have a weekly staff bulletin and a section of it is devoted to 'Bright spots' (see Part 2 Training plans, page 163). We encourage coaches, lead learners and other middle leaders to identify teachers they are working with who are trialing different stretch and challenge strategies and which are having impact on the students they teach. Another way in which staff's work can be celebrated is to host a stretch and challenge TeachMeet and share on a more public platform the good work teachers are doing with regards to their CPD. A more formal way of celebrating staff's achievements is to create a CPD journal, collating all of the best stretch and challenge practice from the school year. If there is room left in the CPD budget, splash out and get it designed and printed professionally; it is an excellent way to show staff how seriously CPD is taken at your school.

Questions for consideration

Above are just some of the issues that the CPD leader will need to grapple with as part of their role. The message is clear: without planning, preparation and strategic thinking, CPD will have minimal impact. To help you make sure the CPD you are offering is effective, consider the following questions:

- How do the stretch and challenge CPD opportunities link to the whole-school development plan?
- Does the stretch and challenge CPD link to past and future training opportunities?
- What impact do I want to see from this CPD opportunity in terms of student achievement?
- How am I going to measure the impact of this CPD opportunity?
- Have I got the most suitable people who are experts in particular approaches to stretch and challenge delivering the CPD?
- Have I got the right people participating in the different stretch and challenge CPD opportunities?
- How will the CPD be followed up to ensure changes in teachers' stretch and challenge practice?
- Is the CPD opportunity the best use of my CPD budget or are there alternatives to consider?

The next section of the book will have a range of stretch and challenge plans for you to consider using with your staff and tweak to suit your own school context.

Teaching tip

Sign up for newsletters from external organisations

An easy way of keeping abreast of the latest research or future CPD opportunities is to sign up for newsletters from external organisations. TES, The Guardian Teacher Network, SSAT, Optimus and Teaching Leaders all have newsletters that are emailed to your inbox. Create an email folder to file away the newsletters and if you read something of interest, share it with your colleagues.

Chapter 1 takeaway

Pass it on

Share blog recommendations

One of the benefits of joining Twitter is that educational bloggers will use Twitter to tweet notifications for new blog posts to read. If you find that you enjoy reading a particular blog, you can subscribe to it and you will be sent an email every time they write a new post. It is so easy to share the link to a blog with colleagues via email. If there are a number of interesting blogs you read, you could save them up and send out a fortnightly notification to all staff at your school with a brief sentence about the content of each of the blog posts.

Share and tweet

Share your ideas about how to make the best use of a school's CPD budget on Twitter using the hashtag #BloomsCPD.

CPD book club recommendation

David Didau, *The Secret of Literacy* (see Bibliography and further reading, page 271). This is a great book that explores how all teachers can challenge students by putting literacy at the heart of all subjects across the curriculum.

Bloggers' corner

David Fawcett's blog is a great read as it is packed with posts about developing his craft. His posts begin with the title 'Can I be that little bit better at...' and he explores his attempts to engage with research and become a better teacher. Visit his blog at: reflectionsofmyteaching.blogspot.co.uk.

To do list:

❏ Talk to your NQTs about what research they read as part of their teacher training

❏ Read *Embedded Formative Assessment* by Dylan Wiliam

❏ Read *The Secret of Literacy* by David Didau

❏ Check out Harry Fletcher-Wood's posts on teacher development: www.improvingteaching.co.uk

❏ Read *The Expert Learner* by Gordon Stobart

❏ Read Chris Chivers' blog on getting the most out of all learners: chrischiversthinks.weebly.com/blog-thinking-aloud

❏ Sign up for newsletters from external organisations to keep abreast of the latest educational news

❏ Round up all of the interesting blog posts you read each fortnight and share with colleagues via an emailed bulletin

❏ Switch the focus away from admin and towards teaching and learning in department meetings

❏ Share your ideas and experiences as widely as possible and be an enthusiastic voice in the staffroom

❏ Tweet your ideas about in-house CPD using the hashtag #BloomsCPD

❏ Read David Fawcett's blog on developing his teaching practice: reflectionsofmyteaching.blogspot.co.uk

Top ten tips to get you started with successful stretch and challenge DIY CPD

We've come to the point where you are now ready to deliver high-quality training on stretch and challenge! Regardless of the position you hold in your school, put yourself forward to help colleagues to develop this aspect of their practice. If you think you're not ready, then take a minute to consider what you've done so far:

- Audited your own practice to get a good starting point about how you challenge all your students
- Read about the different approaches to planning for stretch and challenge
- Engaged with key educational thinkers and their research into stretch and challenge
- Identified specific practical strategies to try out with your classes to raise your students' achievement
- Evaluated the impact of the strategies you have tried with your classes
- Reflected on how you can tweak your practice to get even more out of the strategies you have tried
- Explored different types of CPD to support your colleagues in improving their practice
- Considered how you could collaborate with other schools to develop your own and other colleagues' practice
- Examined the challenges of being the school's CPD leader.

Here are my top ten tips to get you started for successful CPD:

1. Get as many colleagues as you can on board to help you deliver training as you can't do it all by yourself and you will benefit from different perspectives.
2. Be very clear about the objectives for the CPD you are going to deliver and decide in advance how you will measure impact.
3. Make sure the CPD has quick wins to keep people motivated but also

longer-term goals that will lead to a sustained change in practice.

4. Think carefully about the audience for the CPD and build in opportunities to stretch all teachers' thinking.

5. Read as much research about stretch and challenge as possible so you are confident in the messages you are giving staff and staying clear of fads and gimmicks.

6. Remember that the best CPD focuses on student outcomes so bring everything back to how CPD can increase students' chances of experiencing success.

7. Don't lecture participants; instead provide plenty of opportunities for members of staff to talk to each other but be wary of the same voices dominating discussion.

8. Ensure there are clear points for reflection between CPD opportunities so that teachers are learning in between designated CPD time.

9. Identify a follow-up action you expect staff to commit to doing after each CPD opportunity.

10. Get staff to evaluate each CPD opportunity they participate in in order for you to tweak your CPD plans accordingly.

2 Training plans

Overview

In this chapter, you will find a range of plans to use in your school to develop teachers' stretch and challenge provision. It is split into four sections:

1. **15-minute staff briefings**
   There are five 15-minute sessions for the CPD leader to deliver based on a weekly staff briefing. Due to the short nature of the sessions, these are focused on information sharing around some of the strategies from the key educational thinkers discussed in chapter 4.

2. **INSET day**
   This session focuses on introducing all staff to stretch and challenge and sharing approaches from Part 1, chapter 3. Later in the day, teachers break up into smaller groups depending on their level of expertise: beginner, experienced and advanced practice. Time is given over to departments later in the day to implement ideas at a subject-specific level. At the end of the day, all staff will commit to working on an element of their stretch and challenge practice.

3. **Twilight sessions**
   There are four twilight sessions to be run over a term; all staff could attend all four throughout the term if they are run on rotation or members of staff could attend the session most relevant to the aspect of stretch and challenge they are trying to develop The sessions run for one hour and 15 minutes; all sessions are structured around engaging with key educational thinkers, coaching conversations and time to practise and develop a particular strategy to use with students.

4. **Lesson study**
   There are six sessions to attend to complete the lesson study programme. The sessions begin by helping participants to identify their enquiry question and targeted students and engage with relevant research. The subsequent sessions focus on reflecting and refining practice based upon discussion with participating colleagues and the targeted students. The final session is a chance to reflect and celebrate the impact of teachers' lesson study enquiries.

At the start of each of the four sections listed above you will find a planning overview table. Then, each training session includes a planning document and a full set of editable PowerPoint slides that can be downloaded from the online resources site that accompanies this book.

Planning overview

The planning overview provides you with everything you need to know and to prepare for the individual training session. You can also find the template for this document online so you can create your own bespoke overview where necessary, adapting it to your own needs and context.

Below is an annotated example detailing what goes in each section.

Focus	Notes
Facilitators	*Details of who will be involved in the training.*
Session aims	*The key elements that the session aims to fulfil.*
Preparation tasks	*The main things you need to do to prepare for the training session.*
Resources required	*All the resources you need for the training session.*
Follow-up commitment	*Any tasks or documents you will ask the attendees to complete after the training session.*
Potential problems and solutions	*Problems to keep in mind that you might face with the training sessions and recommendations for how to deal with or avoid them.*

Planning document

Each training session is presented in a planning document. This includes a detailed breakdown of every step of the individual training plan, split as detailed below. You can also find an editable version of this table in the online resources.

Focus	Timing	Content
A summary of the stage of the training plan – the key focus or aim (e.g. Introduction of session aims)	*How long you should allow for this part of the training session.*	*Detailed step-by-step guide to what to cover in this section of the training.*

PowerPoint slides

All of the training plans are supported by PowerPoint presentations. These can all be downloaded from the online resources and used as they are or edited and adapted to suit your context. Key slides have been included in the book after the planning document where needed, to help clearly explain the session.

15-minute staff briefings

Staff briefings are often only 15 minutes long, but this does not mean this time cannot be used effectively. Each of these sessions is focused on the use of a particular strategy that students might benefit from the teacher trialling with their class. Reference will be made to a teacher who has already trialled the strategy (called a 'Bright spot') so other teachers can hear first-hand how it has made a positive difference to students. The chosen strategies for these briefings are linked to John Hattie's research; these strategies have proven high effect sizes over 0.4.

Planning overview

Focus	Notes
Facilitators	• The CPD leader will lead the 15-minute briefing. • One teacher with experience of using the particular strategy will share the strategy they have been trialling and explain the impact it has had on their students.
Session aims	1. To understand how to implement a stretch and challenge strategy and how it links to a particular approach to improve student achievement. 2. To listen to the experiences of colleagues who have trialled a particular strategy. 3. To reflect on how to implement this strategy with our own classes.
Preparation tasks	• Email staff at the start of the week to remind them about the staff briefing and share the focus. • Email the member of staff who you want to use as a Bright spot for the briefing. • Check PowerPoint before the session.
Resources required	• PowerPoint presentation. • Teacher's resource linked to the strategy.
Follow-up commitment	• All staff to try this strategy with an individual student, a group of students or a particular class over the next two weeks before the next staff briefing. • Each head of department to share with their SLT line manager a Bright spot from their department.
Potential problems and solutions	**Problem:** Some staff prefer to use the time before school to get ready for the day ahead and may resent having to attend.
	Solution: As the session is only 15 minutes and requires no huge input from staff, it should be an enjoyable and informative session.

Staff briefing 1 planning document

Focus	Timing	Content
Introduction: share the aims of the session	2 minutes	• Share the aims of the briefing using PowerPoint slide 2.
Share the strategy and explain why to trial it	8 minutes	• Show PowerPoint slide 3 with information about 'frequent, low-stakes quizzes' (strategy 9 from chapter 4, page 64). • Explain how this strategy is an example of developing your use of feedback (an approach from Part 1, chapter 3, page 34). • Link this explanation to John Hattie's effect size for feedback. • Ask participants to think about pupils they teach who might benefit from using frequent, low-stakes quizzes.
Listen to how to implement the strategy	5 minutes	• Listen to today's Bright spot share how they implemented the strategy and what impact it has had on their students.

PowerPoint slides

Introduction: share the aims of the session

Aims of the session

1. To understand how to use frequent, low-stakes quizzes to diagnose students' learning.
2. To understand how low-stakes quizzes are one way of generating effective feedback.

Share the strategy and explain why to trial it

Engaging with research

What is frequent, low-stakes quizzing?

Many students hate the idea of tests but that is often because they are seen as high-stakes and competitive. The idea of low-stakes, frequent quizzing is different; it is part of a routine that supports students and teachers in understanding how much has been learnt. Get the students into a routine of knowing that there will be a weekly or fortnightly quiz and that the content in it will be not just present material but material from previous learning. Students can co-construct the quizzes with different students taking responsibility for planning some of the questions.

BLOOMSBURY CPD LIBRARY

Why should you trial this strategy?

- Frequent, low-stakes testing would be a good strategy to trial with a class or group of students for whom you feel you need more regular feedback on what they have learnt.

- It is also a good strategy if you are teaching students who have poor memory retention.

- Feedback has an effect size of 0.82, according to John Hattie. Remember anything higher than 0.4 is generating significant impact on student achievement.

BLOOMSBURY CPD LIBRARY

Staff briefing 2 planning document

Focus	Timing	Content
Introduction: share the aims of the session	2 minutes	• Share the aims of the briefing using PowerPoint slide 2.
Share the strategy and explain why to trial it	8 minutes	• Show PowerPoint slide 3 with information about Socratic discussion (strategy 2 from chapter 4, page 60). • Explain how this strategy is an example of developing your use of questioning and discussion (an approach from Part 1, chapter 4, page 59). • Link this explanation to John Hattie's effect size for classroom discussion. • Ask participants to think about who they teach that might benefit from using Socratic discussion.
Listen to how to implement the strategy	5 minutes	• Listen to today's Bright spot share how they implemented the strategy and what impact it has had on their students.

PowerPoint slides: 15-minute staff briefing 2: Socratic discussion

Introduction: share the aims of the session

Aims of the session

1. To understand how to incorporate Socratic discussion into your lessons to support students in extending their thinking.
2. To understand how Socratic discussion is one way of developing effective classroom discussion.

Share the strategy and explain why to trial it

Engaging with research

What is Socratic discussion?

Another specific model to introduce structured talk to students, focusing on increasing the quality of students' thinking. The process for Socratic discussion is to ask the questions for different reasons. The different types of questions are:

- questions for clarification
- questions that probe assumptions
- questions that probe the evidence
- questions about different perspectives
- questions that probe implications
- questions about the significance of the original question.

Why should you trial this strategy?

- Socratic discussion would be a good strategy to trial with a class or group of students where you feel they need to think in a more sophisticated manner about challenging topics.
- It is also a good strategy if you are teaching students who do not feel comfortable in larger group discussions and do not share their opinions with the rest of the class.
- Feedback has an effect size of 0.75, according to John Hattie. Remember anything higher than 0.4 is generating significant impact on student achievement.

Staff briefing 3 planning document

Focus	Timing	Content
Introduction: share the aims of the session	2 minutes	• Share the aims of the briefing using PowerPoint slide 2.
Share the strategy and explain why to trial it	8 minutes	• Show PowerPoint slide 3 with information about preflight checks (strategy 32 from chapter 4, page 77). • Explain how this strategy is an example of developing students' independence (an approach from Chapter 3, page 36). • Link this explanation to John Hattie's effect size for feedback. • Ask participants to think about who they teach who might benefit from using preflight checklists.
Listen to how to implement the strategy	5 minutes	• Listen to today's Bright spot share how they implemented the strategy and what impact it has had on their students.

PowerPoint slides

Introduction: share the aims of the session

Aims of the session

1. To understand how to incorporate preflight checks into your lessons to support students in extending their thinking.
2. To understand how preflight checks is one way of developing students' independence.

Share the strategy and explain why to trial it

Engaging with research

What are preflight checklists?

Before students hand in a piece of work, get them into a routine of having their 'feedback buddy' complete a preflight checklist. This checklist should work as the success criteria for the piece of work. Students are working to improve each other and take responsibility for ensuring their work is ready for submission. If there are features of the work that aren't good enough or aren't evidenced at all, then there is still time to add to the work before submission.

Why should you trial this strategy?

- Preflight checklists would be a good strategy to trial with a class or group of students where you feel that students often rush their work and are more interested in completing it quickly rather than producing something of quality.
- It is also a good strategy to make the success criteria explicit to students so there is clarity in your expectations.
- Teacher clarity, which clear success criteria and guided practice are examples of, has an effect size of 0.8, according to John Hattie. Remember anything higher than 0.4 is generating significant impact on student achievement.

Staff briefing 4 planning document

Focus	Timing	Content
Introduction: share the aims of the session	2 minutes	• Share the aims of the briefing using PowerPoint slide 2.
Share the strategy and explain why to trial it	8 minutes	• Show PowerPoint slide 3 with information about mind maps (strategy 26 from Chapter 4, page 74). • Explain how this strategy is an example of sharing learning intentions (an approach from Part 1, chapter 3, page 34). • Link this explanation to John Hattie's effect size for concept mapping. • Ask participants who they teach who might benefit from using mind maps.
Listen to how to implement the strategy	5 minutes	• Listen to today's Bright spot share how they implemented the strategy and what impact it has had on their students.

PowerPoint slides

Introduction: share the aims of the session

Aims of the session

1. To understand how to use mind maps to support students in making connections between different learning episodes.
2. To understand how mind maps are one way of making learning intentions relevant and developing conceptual knowledge.

Share the strategy and explain why to trial it

Engaging with research

What are mind maps?

Before beginning a new topic, get students to create a mind map of what they already know. Using this information, test the students so you have accurate baseline data on what they know already; this will help you to plan activities that will truly stretch your students and accelerate their learning. As the unit progresses, encourage students to add to their mind map, making connections between prior and new learning.

Why should you trial this strategy?

- Mind maps would be a good strategy to trial with a class or group of students where you feel that there is a lot of knowledge that a student will have to make sense of to gain conceptual understanding.
- It is also a good strategy to use mind maps to help students identify the bigger picture of learning and remember key information.
- Concept mapping has an effect size of 0.6, according to John Hattie. Remember anything higher than 0.4 is generating significant impact on student achievement.

Staff briefing 5 planning document

Focus	Timing	Content
Introduction: share the aims of the session	2 minutes	• Share the aims of the briefing using PowerPoint slide 2.
Share the strategy and explain why to trial it	8 minutes	• Show PowerPoint slide 3 with information about a set of task instructions (strategy 20 from chapter 4, page 71). • Explain how this strategy is an example of developing scaffolding resources (an approach from Part 1, chapter 3, page 33). • Ask participants who they teach who might benefit from creating a set of task instructions.
Listen to how to implement the strategy	5 minutes	• Listen to today's Bright spot share how they implemented the strategy and what impact it has had on their students.

PowerPoint slides

Introduction: share the aims of the session

Aims of the session

1. To understand how to create a set of task instructions to support students in working independently for longer periods of time.
2. To understand how written task instructions are one way of keeping students on track and showing resilience when they work through a task.

BLOOMSBURY CPD LIBRARY

Share the strategy and explain why to trial it

Engaging with research

What is a set of task instructions?

If a task requires students to work on it for an extended period of time, then one way you can support students is to provide a clear set of instructions for success. If students are more confident, they can always write their own set of instructions that they can tick off as they go along. Encourage students to write out the instructions in small steps using imperatives. Adding visuals to a set of task instructions also helps students who struggle to process information.

BLOOMSBURY CPD LIBRARY

Why should you trial this strategy?

- A set of written task instructions would be a good strategy to trial with a class or group of students where you feel that they are reliant on you and struggle to work independently.
- It is also a good strategy to use written task instructions to help students break down a challenging task into manageable chunks and self-regulate.
- Scaffolding, which chunked task instructions is an example of, has an effect size of 0.53, according to John Hattie. Remember anything higher than 0.4 is generating significant impact on student achievement.

BLOOMSBURY CPD LIBRARY

INSET day

The INSET day has to have the right balance of the whole school coming together and working towards a common goal but also acknowledging that participants have different levels of expertise. Consequently, sessions 3 and 4 that follow are split into beginner, experienced and advanced groups; the core message of how the school wants to develop stretch and challenge provision remains the same in each group but the way in which these aims are achieved differs according to the level of expertise of the attendees. Session 5 is department-based as this allows the general principles from the earlier sessions to be embedded into department practice and gives participants an opportunity to reflect on how different approaches and strategies will need to be tweaked for their subject area.

Planning overview

Focus	Notes
Facilitators	• The CPD leader is most likely to lead the opening keynote and audit (introduction and session 1), the explanation of different pedagogical foci for approaching stretch and challenge (session 2), and the reflection and evaluation session (session 6).
	• Lead learners should lead the three option sessions in session 3 as well as facilitate the coaching conversations in session 4.
	• Heads of department will lead session 5 in the afternoon focusing on scheme of work development.
Session aims	1. To understand the different pedagogical approaches to stretch and challenge.
	2. To share effective strategies based on research.
	3. To reflect on how to implement these strategies with our own classes.
	4. To modify current schemes of work in light of approaches and strategies discussed in earlier sessions.
Preparation tasks	• Email all staff a week in advance asking them to choose which of the options in sessions 3 and 4 they will attend.
	• Email the questionnaire to all staff in advance to look over so they know what to expect.
	• Organise how you will set up the room you will be using, noting where you want participants to sit.
	• Print off a seating plan so participants can move quickly to where they need to be.
	• Print off the participant list for the two option sessions (sessions 3 and 4).
	• Print off evaluation forms and next steps documents for staff to complete.
	• Check video links are working.

Focus	Notes
Resources required	• PowerPoint presentation. • Self-evaluation questionnaire from chapter 2 (page 18 – also available to download from the online resources) for each member of staff. • Seating plan. • Audio equipment and connection to the Internet. • Video clips for each session. • Sugar paper and marker pens for group. • Sets of laminated cards for each group, with each card describing a different stretch and challenge approach.
Follow-up commitment	• All staff to identify an approach and strategy to focus on with one class for their coaching partnership or Lesson study. • Each department to hand over their curriculum questionnaire to their SLT line manager. • Heads of department to lead their team on scheme of work development in the next department meeting.
Potential problems and solutions	**Problem:** Some staff dislike INSETs because they have a one-size-fits-all feel. **Solution:** Optional sessions in sessions 3 and 4 should overcome this and the significant amount of time working in their own department should be useful time to apply ideas in a specific subject context.

INSET day planning document

Focus	Timing	Content
Introduction: set the tone, show the sessions for the day and share the aims for the INSET	15 minutes	• Show the plan for the day so everyone is clear about the different sessions. • Share the aims of the INSET. • Ask participants if there are any other aims they would like to add. • Ask participants to discuss in their department groups: the school context and the particular barriers to learning that they come across.
Session 1: Complete individual stretch and challenge audit	45 minutes	• Introduce the stretch and challenge audit and hand out the stretch and challenge audit to each participant (self-evaluation questionnaire in chapter 2). • Go through each question and explain how to complete the audit. • Get participants to complete the quick self-evaluation part of the questionnaire. • Participants are encouraged to reflect on their area for development and share this with colleagues they are sitting with.

Focus	Timing	Content
Session 2: Explanation of approaches to stretch and challenge	30 minutes	• Hand out cards with different approaches to stretch and challenge, as explored in chapter 3, to small groups. • Get participants to discuss which approaches they already make use of with their classes and to consider the pros and cons of each approach. • Get participants to work in their department groups to explore which approaches are embedded in their department practice and which ones need further consideration.
Session 3: Option sessions: **A Beginner (developing practice)** **B Experienced (securing practice)** **C Advanced (embedding practice)** **Introduce practical strategies based on key educational thinkers' research**	1 hour	**The structure of each option session is the same but the research focus is different. The reading and strategies for each session are differentiated so that the ideas in Option C require some expertise in stretch and challenge.** • Option A focuses on John Hattie and Dylan Wiliam's research into the importance of sharing learning intentions, success criteria and levels of challenge in task design (pages 76-77). • Option B focuses on John Hattie, Dylan Wiliam and Carol Dweck's research into the importance of activating peer support, collaborative learning and scaffolding students' learning to build resilience (pages 77-78). • Option C focuses on John Hattie, Dylan Wiliam and Ron Berger's research into creating a culture of learning which focuses on giving and receiving effective feedback from peers and the teacher to improve learning (pages 61-67).
Session 3: Option **A Beginner: Setting high expectations and challenging all learners.**	1 hour	• Share the aims of the session with participants. • Display discussion questions to generate thinking about setting high expectations. • Watch video clips of John Hattie and Dylan Wiliam discussing their research on the importance of sharing learning intentions, success criteria and levels of challenge in task design. • Further discussion time to explore the research after watching the video clips.

Focus	Timing	Content
		• Participants complete practice tasks based on specific strategies to use in class based on research: designing success criteria for a task and creating three levels of challenge for a task. • Participants reflect and evaluate the session and set up the coaching conversations for the following session.
Option B Experienced: Supporting students to become autonomous learners.	1 hour	• Share the aims of the session with participants. • Display discussion questions to generate thinking on supporting students to become autonomous learners. • Watch video clips of John Hattie, Dylan Wiliam and Carol Dweck discussing their research on the importance of activating peer support, collaborative learning and scaffolding students' learning to build resilience. • Further discussion time to explore the research after watching the video clips. • Participants complete practice tasks based on specific strategies to use in class based on research: designing a series of scaffolds for a challenging piece of work and a collaborative learning task. • Participants reflect and evaluate the session and set up the coaching conversations for the following session.
Option C Advanced: Creating an ethic of excellence in your students	1 hour	• Share the aims of the session with participants. • Display discussion questions to generate thinking about creating an ethic of excellence in your students. • Watch video clips of John Hattie, Ron Berger, Dylan Wiliam and Carol Dweck discussing their research on the importance of giving and receiving effective feedback from peers and the teacher to improve learning. • Further discussion time to explore the research after watching the video clips. • Participants complete practice tasks based on specific strategies to use in class based on research: creating a charter of excellence and designing step-by-step feedback to give students based on refining a piece of work. • Participants reflect and evaluate the session and set up the coaching conversations for the following session.

Focus	Timing	Content
BREAK	15 minutes	
Session 4: Coaching session based on specific strategies linked to the previous session	1 hour	• Share research into why coaching is an effective method to develop teachers' practice. • Show the participants the GROW model of coaching with suggested questions to use as conversation prompts. • In the same discussion from the previous session, each participant is coached through a particular strategy based on research from earlier that they could use to develop their own stretch and challenge provision.
LUNCH	1 hour	
Session 5: Modify existing scheme of work in departments	1 hour 45 minutes	• Departments decide on a scheme of work to focus on during the session. • All departments are given copies of the guidance table, which acts as a scaffold for the session to judge the effectiveness of the stretch and challenge provision in the scheme of work. • Departments complete the table and assign RAG ratings to each approach to stretch and challenge in the scheme of work. • Departments assign actions to improve the scheme of work based on any approaches that have been rated as amber or red.
Session 6: Reflection and evaluation of the INSET	15 minutes	• Return to the aims of the INSET and remind participants what the INSET has set out to achieve. • Hand out evaluation forms to participants so that they reflect and evaluate their knowledge and set their next steps to develop their approach to stretch and challenge.

PowerPoint slides

Introduction session: Set the tone, show sessions for the day and share aims for the INSET

Plan for the day

Time	Activity
8.45 – 9.00	**Introduction** Introduce INSET aims and link to the school development plan
9.00 – 9.45	**Session 1** Staff audit of stretch and challenge practice with follow-up discussion
9.45 – 10.15	**Session 2** Explain approaches to stretch and challenge
10.15 – 11.15	**Session 3** Option A: Setting high expectations and challenging all learners Option B: Supporting students to become autonomous learners Option C: Creating an ethic of excellence in your students
11.15 – 11.30	**Break**
11.30 – 12.30	**Session 4** Coaching conversations based on ideas from session 1
12.30 – 1.30	**Lunch**
1.30 – 3.15	**Session 5** Department time modifying scheme of work
3.15 – 3.30	**Session 6** Reflection and evaluation

INSET aims

1. To understand the different pedagogical approaches to stretch and challenge.
2. To share effective strategies based on research.
3. To reflect on how to implement these strategies with our own classes.
4. To modify current schemes of work in light of approaches and strategies discussed in earlier sessions.

Session 1: Complete individual stretch and challenge audit

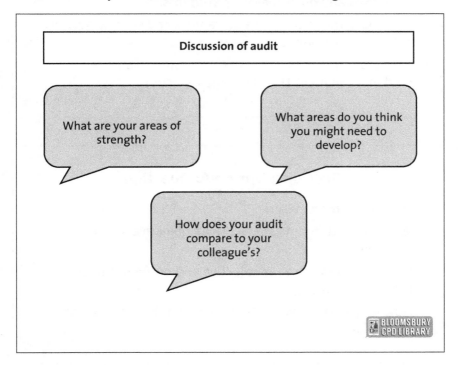

The slides for Session 2 are available on the companion website for the book (www.bloomsbury.com/CPD-library-stretch-and-challenge). More detail can also be found in the INSET day planning document on page 179.

Session 3: Option A Beginner: Setting high expectations and challenging all learners

---

Session 3 Option A: Aims

Developing stretch and challenge practice

Setting high expectations and challenging all learners.

Aims:

- To explore the importance of framing and sharing lesson objectives and outcomes with students.
- To explore the importance of framing and sharing success criteria with students.
- To explore the importance of task design to ensure all students can meet their learning objective.

BLOOMSBURY CPD LIBRARY

Session 3 Option A: Questions

Questions for discussion:

- What is the difference between an objective and an outcome?
- How do you frame your objective and outcomes to ensure they offer challenge?
- How do you share your objective and outcomes with your students?

BLOOMSBURY CPD LIBRARY

Session 3 Option A

What are the possible issues with framing your outcomes in this way?

Learning objective

To understand what is meant by the term 'stretch and challenge'.

Learning outcomes

All participants will identify different ways of planning effective stretch and challenge.

Most participants will compare the different approaches and consider the pros and cons of each approach.

Some participants will judge which approaches are most effective taking into consideration the specific students they teach.

Session 3 Option A: Practice task

Think of a topic you are going to teach next week and a piece of work you would assess and give feedback on. Construct the success criteria for it now.

After, you will have to explain to the person sitting next to you the following:

- What is the assessment?
- What would be the ingredients of an excellent example of this assessment?
- How have you broken this down to help the students unpick how to get there?
- What choices have you made visually to help the students make use of the criteria and understand how to challenge themselves?

Session 3 Option A: Practice task

Think of a topic you are going to teach next week and the key learning objective. Consider the range of learners in your class. What levels of challenge can you build into a task to help all students meet their learning objective?

After, you will have to explain to the person sitting next to you the following:

- What are the fundamentals of the task that you would expect all students to do?
- How can you tweak the task to offer further support for those students who may struggle?
- How can you tweak the task to offer further stretch for those students who are finding it too easy?

Remember that offering more of the same is not stretching students cognitively. Likewise, making students do something easy isn't supporting them; it's lowering your expectations.

Session 3 Option B: Experienced: Supporting students to become autonomous learners

Session 3 Option B: Aims

Securing stretch and challenge practice

Supporting students to become autonomous learners.

Aims:
- To explore the importance of collaborative working in developing independence from the teacher.
- To explore the importance of developing resilience when students are struggling.
- To explore the importance of scaffolds and when to use them to support students.

Session 3 Option B: Questions

Questions for discussion:
- Why should we want students to work independently?
- Why should we want students to work collaboratively?
- What role does the teacher have in supporting students to become autonomous?

Session 3 Option B

What are the possible issues with this task information sheet for students?

Task information

You are going to research topic X.

You can work by yourself or in groups.

You can use any resources including the Internet.

You will need to state the sources of your information.

At the end of the lesson, you will present your research to the rest of the class.

Session 3 Option B: Practice task

Think of a topic you are going to teach next week and the learning outcomes. Modify this learning so that it becomes a collaborative learning episode as opposed to students working individually directed by the teacher.

After, you will have to explain to the person sitting next to you the following:

- What was the original task?
- How are you establishing group goals?
- How are you establishing individual accountability?
- How have you structured and scaffolded the task so that students have some autonomy and are not looking for you to spoon-feed them?

Session 3 Option B: Practice task

Think of a topic you are going to teach and something that students normally find quite difficult to do. Create a series of scaffolds that students can use to help them work independently and persevere when they begin to struggle.

After, you will have to explain to the person sitting next to you the following:

- What scaffold have you provided for students who are really out of their comfort zone and would normally require a lot of teacher input?
- What scaffold have you provided for students who are anxious about starting but are fine once they've got started?
- What strategies will you use to ensure that some students don't rely on the scaffold if they are capable of working without one?

BLOOMSBURY
CPD LIBRARY

Session 3: Option C Advanced: Creating an ethic of excellence in your students

---

Session 3 Option C: Aims

Embedding stretch and challenge practice
Creating an ethic of excellence in your students.

Aims:
- To explore the importance of sharing examples of excellence with students.
- To explore the importance of creating a culture of critique with students.
- To explore the importance of students taking responsibility for developing their own learning.

BLOOMSBURY
CPD LIBRARY

Session 3 Option C: Questions

Questions for discussion:

- What are the hallmarks of an excellent piece of work in your subject?
- What are the difficulties in getting students to self- and peer-assess?
- How can students be forced to take greater responsibility for their own learning?

Session 3 Option C

What are the possible issues with this task guidance?

Assessment guidance

You are going to complete a piece of work about X.

Look at the mark scheme for this task.

Think carefully about what you are going to have to include in your work to reach your target grade.

You will have 45 minutes to complete the work.

I will be marking this work so give it your best effort.

Session 3 Option C: Practice task

Think about the expectations you share with your students about what you want them to be like in your lessons. Consider what language you would need to use to make explicit to students that you are only interested in them creating excellent work. Draft out a set of
subject-specific expectations to share with a class you teach.

After, you will have to explain to the person sitting next to you the following:

- What would an excellent student in your subject be able to know and do?
- What have you prioritised as important?
- What language have you used to show that excellence can be achieved in your class?
- What would you have to change in your current classroom practice and routines to enable a culture of excellence?

Session 3 Option C: Practice task

Think about an assessment in a scheme of work you teach. Begin with the end and describe all the features that would make the work excellent. Then break down the stages to give specific feedback to help a student get to that point of excellence.

After, you will have to explain to the person sitting next to you the following:

- What are the hallmarks of excellence?
- Which aspects do students struggle with normally?
- How can this feedback help them to overcome these moments of difficulty?

Session 4: Coaching session based on specific strategies linked to the previous session

---

Session 4: Coaching conversations

Aims:

- To reflect on your current practice for providing challenge for all learners.
- To coach another member of staff to move forward with their stretch and challenge provision to improve student outcomes.
- To receive coaching from another member of staff to move forward with your stretch and challenge provision to improve student outcomes.

BLOOMSBURY CPD LIBRARY

Research into effectiveness of coaching

'The reflection promoted by effective mentoring and coaching approaches in turn encourages a collaborative learning culture in organisations. For schools, this is particularly important, as it may alleviate some of the sense of professional isolation. Mentoring and coaching activities may be more influential when they "fit" the wider context of an organisation, and/ or when they are part of a wider programme of professional development.'

(Lord et al. (2008), *Mentoring and Coaching for Professionals: A Study of the Research Evidence*, NFER, p. viii)

BLOOMSBURY CPD LIBRARY

Tips for effective coaching conversations

- Do not give your partner the answers!
- Actively listen to what they are saying and read between the lines.
- Ask open-ended questions that will encourage them to reflect on their practice.
- Encourage them to consider a range of options.
- Get them to commit to trying something and articulate what impact they hope it will have on the students.

Deciding on a focus

Think back to the first session.
What was your takeaway from the session – something that grabbed you as important about your practice.
What do you want to focus on with a particular class?
This is going to form the basis of your coaching conversation.
Share now with your coaching partner what you have chosen.

The GROW model

GOAL	REALITY	OPTIONS	WAY FORWARD
What do they want to achieve? Why do they want to achieve this?	What are the issues they are facing that are hindering their goals? What have they tried already?	What have they thought about that they could try? What do they think are the pros and cons of each option?	What are they going to commit to trying? What do they hope will be the impact?

The GROW model – stretch and challenge

GOAL	REALITY	OPTIONS	WAY FORWARD
What aspect of stretch and challenge do you want to work on? Can you describe what you would like to see and hear from your students?	Where are you at now with your current practice? What is working well right now? What barriers to learning are you encountering from your students?	What have you tried already? What might you try first? What else could you try if that doesn't work? Is there any research you've engaged with that you could use?	What actions are you going to commit to moving forward? What support will you need to make it happen? How will you know if it has had successful impact?

Session 5: Modify existing scheme of work in departments

Does the scheme of work have ...	RAG rating	If amber or red, actions to turn green	Lead person making this change
Clear, progressive and challenging learning intentions?			
Opportunities for independent learning?			
Challenging questions and structured discussion?			
Challenging tasks that are accessible to all learners?			
Resources that support students to learn challenging material?			
Opportunities for collaborative learning?			
Structured and regular feedback and reflection time?			
Clear provision for developing academic language?			
Challenging homework tasks to extend learning?			

Session 6: Reflection and evaluation

Question	Response
What was your current level of knowledge about stretch and challenge before today's INSET?	
What was the most valuable aspect of today's INSET?	
What have you learnt today that you had not considered previously?	
What are you going to do differently with your students after today's INSET?	
What further information or training would you like to participate in?	

Twilight sessions

This section includes four twilight sessions:

1. Stretching students' thinking
2. Developing students' language
3. Improving students' memories
4. Increasing students' commitment to learning

It is a good idea to run all four of these sessions four times over a term so that it is possible for all members of staff to attend all four sessions by the end of a term. The session structure remains consistent to ensure quality delivery and coherence of approach from the lead learners delivering the sessions.

Each session begins with introducing the ideas of key educational thinkers before translating the research into practical strategies to use with students. There is time set aside in each session for participants to engage in a coaching conversation using the GROW model (Goal, Reality, Options, Way forward – see INSET day PowerPoint slide 39, page 194) and then following up with practice time and reflection.

Planning overview

Focus	Notes
Facilitators	• Each twilight session will be delivered by a lead learner who has been identified as having excellent knowledge of stretch and challenge. • The lead learner will have carried out extensive reading around the particular focus of the session and will be able to share this knowledge and support teachers in selecting appropriate strategies to try with their students.
Session aims	1. To engage with the ideas of key educational thinkers linked to the focus area of stretch and challenge. 2. To share effective strategies based on research. 3. To reflect on how to implement these strategies with our own classes. 4. To modify existing practice to improve the outcomes of a particular class or a targeted group of students.
Preparation tasks	• Email staff a week in advance of each twilight session to share which session they have been allocated. • Liaise with the four lead learners who are running the twilight sessions to check there are no issues with their session outline and resources. • Email a participant list to the lead learners so they know who to expect in each session. • Print off wider reading handouts for each session. • Print off evaluation form and next steps document for staff to complete.

Focus	Notes
Resources required	• PowerPoint presentations. • Key educational thinkers' summaries for each session. • Participant lists. • Audio equipment and connection to the Internet. • Sugar paper and marker pens for each group. • Evaluation forms.
Follow-up commitment	• After the four sessions have been attended, teachers will commit to trialling two suggested strategies with their students. • This will then feed into department meetings the following term in which there will be a standing agenda item where different members of staff share what they are trying and reflect on the impact it is having.
Potential problems and solutions	**Problem:** In the twilight sessions there will be different levels of experience amongst staff. **Solution:** The lead learner needs to draw upon and share with the group, the experiences of different staff members and ensure coaching pairings are carefully thought through. More experienced teachers need to feel that their expertise is valued so ask them questions and ensure everyone is involved in discussion.

Twilight 1 planning document: Stretching students' thinking

Focus	Timing	Content
Set the tone and share aims of the session	5 minutes	• Start off the training by sharing the session plan and aims. • Ask participants if there are any other aims they would like to add. • Participants share their definition of what they consider to be 'deep thinking'.
Wider reading task based on summaries of key educational thinkers' research	10 minutes	• Put participants into pairs to investigate two of the educational thinkers from chapter 4: one of each pair is allocated Robin Alexander (page 59) and the other Dylan Wiliam (page 76). • Each participant is given a handout to read about their educational thinker (from online) and they highlight the key ideas. • Then, back in their pairs, participants share with their partner the key ideas they have identified.
Discussion on different ideas from the key educational thinkers relating back to own school context	10 minutes	• Display the debate questions on PowerPoint slide 5. • Participants discuss in their pairs the ideas of Alexander and Wiliam, linking them to their own context.

Focus	Timing	Content
Introduce specific strategies based on research of key educational thinkers	10 minutes	• Display the practical strategies based on the research of Alexander and Wiliam (see also chapter 4, pages 59 & 76): Alexander – Philosophy for Children; Wiliam – Students design their own tests. • For each strategy, display the thinking prompts that follow for consideration by the participants.
Coaching conversations on possible strategies to try out for own class context	15 minutes	• Show the participants the GROW model of coaching with suggested questions to use as conversation prompts. • In the same pairs from the start of the session, each participant coaches their partner through their chosen strategy to stretch students' thinking using the question prompts.
Practice task focusing on applying these strategies	15 minutes	• Introduce the two practice tasks. • Participants select the strategy that they think will be most useful for developing the level of challenge with a particular class or group of students following their coaching conversation, and complete the practice task.
Reflection and evaluation of the session	10 minutes	• Return to the aims of the session and remind participants what the session has set out to achieve. • Participants select a potential class or group of students to trial the strategy with. However, no final decisions will be made until all four sessions have been attended. • Hand out evaluation forms to participants so that they reflect and evaluate their knowledge and set their next steps to stretch students' thinking.

PowerPoint slides: Twilight 1: Stretching students' thinking
Set the tone and share aims of the session

Aims of the session

1. To engage with the ideas of Robin Alexander and Dylan Wiliam on how to challenge students.
2. To share effective strategies based on research about how to stretch students' thinking.
3. To reflect on how to implement these strategies with our own classes.
4. To modify existing practice to improve the outcomes of a particular class or a targeted group of students.

What is deep thinking?

How would you identify if a student was able to think deeply?

What impact does being able to think deeply have on how a student participates and interacts in class?

Take a couple of minutes to discuss these questions with the person sitting next to you.

Discussion on different ideas from the key educational thinkers relating back to own school context

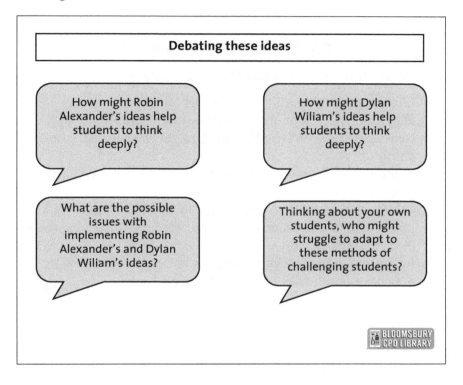

Introduce specific strategies based on research of key educational thinkers

---

Implementing Alexander's ideas

Practical strategy: Philosophy for Children (P4C)

- Choose a stimulus which provokes thought (e.g. a video clip, a photograph or a statement).
- Give students silent thinking time to get to grips with the stimulus.
- Students put forward different questions they would like to discuss and debate.
- The teacher facilitates a discussion in which the students participate and build on others' contributions, justifying their opinions with reasons.
- At the end of the session, students share how their opinions may have changed as a result of the dialogue.

Implementing Wiliam's ideas

Practical strategy: Students design their own tests

- The aim is for students to create tests for each other so the teacher can judge whether they have a full understanding of the material being studied.
- The teacher first models good and bad questions to include in the test.
- Students will need to know the answers to the questions before they can administer the test for their partner so this is an effective way of enabling the student to know whether they've mastered the content.

Our students

Take a minute to think about a student, a group of students or a class you teach who might benefit from this strategy.

Why have you chosen these particular students?

Be ready to share your selected students with the rest of the group.

Practice task focusing on applying these strategies

The GROW model – stretching students' thinking

GOAL	REALITY	OPTIONS	WAY FORWARD
Which strategy do you want to try out? Which students might benefit? How might these students benefit from this strategy?	What barriers to learning are you encountering from these students? How are these barriers affecting their ability to think deeply about ideas discussed in your class?	What have you tried already? What were the pros and cons to what you've tried? How might this strategy be better?	What actions are you going to commit to moving forward? What support will you need to make it happen? How will you know if it has had successful impact?

Practice tasks

Philosophy for Children	Students designing tests
• Think about something you are going to teach where you could use Philosophy for Children. • Decide on a range of stimuli you are going to use to start off the Philosophy for Children session. • Then outline the rules and expectations of the session that you will share with students.	• Think about an assessment you would create for students at the end of a topic. • Instead of using this assessment, think about when students could design their own test and write the mark scheme for it. • Create a set of instructions that you will give to students to help them carry out this task.

Reflection and evaluation of the session

Reflection and evaluation

Question	Response
What strategies do you already routinely use with students to develop the quality of their thinking?	
What did you want to get out of today's session?	
How has today's session developed your understanding of how to develop students' thinking?	
What specific changes are you going to commit to making after today's session?	
What further information or training would you like the lead learner to offer to support you in achieving these changes?	

Twilight 2 planning document: Developing students' language

Focus	Timing	Content
Set the tone and share aims of the session	5 minutes	• Start off the training by sharing the session plan and aims. • Ask participants if there are any other aims they would like to add. • Participants share their understanding of the link between use of language and success in learning.
Wider reading task based on summaries of key educational thinkers' research	10 minutes	• Put participants into pairs to investigate two of the educational thinkers from chapter 4: one of each pair is allocated Robert Marzano (page 71) and the other Doug Lemov (page 68). • Each participant is given a handout to read about their educational thinker (from online) and they highlight the key ideas. • Then, back in their pairs, participants share with their partner the key ideas they have identified.
Discussion on different ideas from the key educational thinkers relating back to own school context	10 minutes	• Display the debate questions on PowerPoint slide 5. • Participants discuss in their pairs the ideas of Marzano and Lemov, linking them to their own context.
Introduce specific strategies based on research of key educational thinkers	10 minutes	• Display the practical strategies based on the research of Robert Marzano and Doug Lemov (see also chapter 4, pages 70 & 72): Marzano – Vocabulary notebooks to support vocabulary upgrades; Lemov – Right is right: Oral rehearsal. • For each strategy, display the thinking prompts that follow for consideration by the participants.
Coaching conversations on possible strategies to try out for own class context	15 minutes	• Show the participants the GROW model of coaching with suggested questions to use as conversation prompts. • In the same pairs from the start of the session, each participant coaches their partner through a particular strategy they could use to develop students' language.

Focus	Timing	Content
Practice task focusing on applying these strategies	15 minutes	• Introduce the two practice tasks. • Participants select the strategy that they think will be most useful for developing the level of challenge with a particular class or group of students following their coaching conversation, and complete the practice task.
Reflection and evaluation of the session	10 minutes	• Return to the aims of the session and remind participants what the session has set out to achieve. • Participants select a potential class or group of students to trial the strategy with. However, no final decisions will be made until all four sessions have been attended. • Hand out evaluation forms to participants so that they reflect and evaluate their knowledge and set their next steps to develop students' use of language.

PowerPoint slides: Twilight 2: Developing students' language

Set the tone and share aims of the session

Aims of the session

1. To engage with the ideas of Robert Marzano and Doug Lemov on how to stretch students.

2. To share effective strategies based on research about how to develop students' language.

3. To reflect on how to implement these strategies with our own classes.

4. To modify existing practice to improve the outcomes of a particular class or a targeted group of students.

Why is language critical for success?

How would you identify if a student has good language skills?

What impact does having good language skills have on a student's chance of success across the curriculum?

Take a couple of minutes to discuss these questions with the person sitting next to you.

Discussion on different ideas from the key educational thinkers relating back to own school context

Debating these ideas

How might Robert Marzano's ideas help students to develop their academic language?

How might Doug Lemov's ideas help teachers to make language central to students' learning?

What are the possible issues with implementing Robert Marzano's and Doug Lemov's ideas?

Thinking about your own students, who might struggle to adapt to these methods of developing language?

Introduce specific strategies based on research of key educational thinkers

---

Implementing Marzano's ideas

Practical strategy: Vocabulary notebooks to support vocabulary upgrades

- Give each student a vocabulary notebook with one page for each word.
- Divide the page into: the word; an example; a sentence using the word; a visual representation; synonyms; antonyms.
- Give students a passage of text with easy words highlighted. Ask students to replace these words with more academic (tier 2) choices or technical (tier 3) choices.
- Students share their new versions of the text with their peers
- You can then select a few examples and use them as a stimulus for whole-class discussion.

Implementing Lemov's ideas

Practical strategy: Right is right – Oral rehearsal

- To increase the quality of students' responses, give them some time to work out how they will respond to your question and practise an oral rehearsal.
- Randomly select a handful of students to stand up and verbalise their response.
- Students have to decide which answer or answers are 100% correct commenting on the content and the vocabulary used.
- The teacher's role is to draw out some of the subtleties in the students' responses rather than to say straight away which answers are best.

Our students

Take a minute to think about a student, a group of students or a class you teach who might benefit from this strategy.

Why have you chosen these particular students?

Be ready to share your selected students with the rest of the group.

Practice task focusing on applying these strategies

The GROW model – developing students' language

GOAL	REALITY	OPTIONS	WAY FORWARD
Which strategy do you want to try out?	What barriers to learning are you encountering from these students?	What have you tried already?	What actions are you going to commit to moving forward?
Which students might benefit?		What were the pros and cons to what you've tried?	
How might these students benefit from this strategy?	How are these barriers affecting their ability to think deeply about ideas discussed in your class?	How might this strategy be better?	What support will you need to make it happen?
			How will you know if it has had successful impact?

Practice tasks

Vocabulary notebooks and vocabulary upgrades	Right is right – oral rehearsal
• Think about something you are going to teach where you will be introducing a lot of new terminology. • Decide on the key words you are going to teach and design a page template for the notebook. • Then practise writing passages linked to the content you will be teaching where students can upgrade certain words using their notebook.	• Think about something you are going to teach where you could set up a class discussion. • Decide on the questions you want students to respond to during the discussion. • Create a resource to support students in using the correct language when responding to these questions.

Reflection and evaluation of the session

Reflection and evaluation

Question	Response
What strategies do you already routinely use with students to develop students' use of language?	
What did you want to get out of today's session?	
How has today's session developed your understanding of how to improve students' academic language?	
What specific changes are you going to commit to making after today's session?	
What further information or training would you like the lead learner to offer to support you in achieving these changes?	

Twilight 3 planning document: Improving students' memories

Focus	Timing	Content
Set the tone and share aims of the session	5 minutes	• Start off the training by sharing the session plan and aims. • Ask participants if there are any other aims they would like to add. • Participants share their thoughts on the link between excellent memory and building knowledge and understanding.
Wider reading task based on summaries of key educational thinkers' research	10 minutes	• Put participants into groups of three to investigate the research of key educational thinkers from chapter 4: one from each group is allocated Daniel Willingham (page 78), another Graham Nuthall (page 73) and the third Peter Brown, Henry Roediger and Mark McDaniel (page 62). • Each participant is given a handout to read about their educational thinker or thinkers (from online) and they highlight the key ideas. • Participants share the key ideas in their groups of three.
Discussion on different ideas from the key educational thinkers relating back to own school context	10 minutes	• Display the debate questions on PowerPoint slide 5. • In their groups of three, participants discuss the ideas of Willingham, Nuthall and Brown, Roediger and McDaniel, linking them to their own context.
Introduce specific strategies based on research of key educational thinkers	10 minutes	• Display the practical strategies based on the researchers discussed (see also chapter 4, page 57): Willingham – Plan for forgetting; Nuthall – Revisit threshold concepts; Brown et al.– Knowledge organisers. • For each strategy, display the thinking prompts that follow for consideration by the participants.
Coaching conversations on possible strategies to try out for own class context	15 minutes	• Show the participants the GROW model of coaching with suggested questions to use as conversation prompts. • In the same threes from the start of the session, each participant coaches their partner through a particular strategy they could use to improve students' memories.

Focus	Timing	Content
Practice task focusing on applying these strategies	15 minutes	• Introduce the practice tasks. • Participants select the strategy that they think will be most useful for developing the level of challenge with a particular class or group of students following their coaching conversation, and complete the practice task.
Reflection and evaluation of the session	10 minutes	• Return to the aims of the session and remind participants what the session has set out to achieve. • Participants select a potential class or group of students to trial the strategy with. However, no final decisions will be made until all four sessions have been attended. • Hand out evaluation forms to participants so that they reflect and evaluate their knowledge and set their next steps to improving students' memories.

PowerPoint slides: Twilight 3: Improving students' memories

Set the tone and share aims of the session

Aims of the session

1. To engage with the ideas about memory from the texts *Why Don't Students Like School?*, *The Hidden Lives of Learners* and *Make It Stick*.
2. To share effective strategies based on research about how to improve students' memories.
3. To reflect on how to implement these strategies with our own classes.
4. To modify existing practice to improve the outcomes of a particular class or a targeted group of students.

Why is memory so important?

How would you identify if a student has a good working memory and good long-term memory retention?

What role does memory have in ensuring students are able to develop their knowledge and understanding?

Take a couple of minutes to discuss these questions with the person sitting next to you.

BLOOMSBURY CPD LIBRARY

Discussion on different ideas from the key educational thinkers relating back to own school context

Debating these ideas

How might Daniel Willingham's ideas and the ideas from the authors of *Make It Stick* help students to improve their memory?

How might Graham Nuthall's ideas help teachers to change the way they plan their lessons?

What are the possible issues with implementing these ideas for improving memory retention?

Thinking about your own students, who might struggle to adapt to these methods of improving memory?

BLOOMSBURY CPD LIBRARY

Introduce specific strategies based on research of key educational thinkers

---

Implementing Willingham's ideas

Practical strategy: Plan for forgetting

- Use homework time to assign students' previously-learnt topics and challenge them to revise the material and take short quizzes to test how much they remember.

- The larger the gap between teaching the content and then taking the test, the harder the brain has to work to retrieve the information.

Implementing Nuthall's ideas

Practical strategy: Revisit threshold concepts

- Using Nuthall's formula that students need to encounter a new idea in full at least three times for it to be stored into their long-term memory, create opportunities for students to revisit ideas throughout the topic.

- Decide in advance what the threshold concepts are for the topic the students are studying and encourage them to reflect on what they understand about these threshold concepts at different points using learning logs or their mind maps.

Implementing Brown, Roediger and McDaniel's ideas

Practical strategy: Knowledge organisers

- Students create knowledge organisers for new information you have shared with them. Depending on how often you see your classes, this might be every week, fortnight or half term.

- The knowledge organiser is a tool that supports students in remembering the key knowledge they need to know before they can move on to a new concept or topic.

- The knowledge organiser should ideally fit onto one page of A4.

- Students build up a bank of knowledge organisers over time – a much better use of time than reading over notes.

Our students

Take a minute to think about a student, a group of students or a class you teach who might benefit from this strategy.

Why have you chosen these particular students?

Be ready to share your selected students with the rest of the group.

Practice task focusing on applying these strategies

The GROW model – improving students' memories

GOAL	REALITY	OPTIONS	WAY FORWARD
Which strategy do you want to try out? Which students might benefit? How might these students benefit from this strategy?	What barriers to learning are you encountering from these students? How are these barriers affecting their ability to think deeply about ideas discussed in your class?	What have you tried already? What were the pros and cons to what you've tried? How might this strategy be better?	What actions are you going to commit to moving forward? What support will you need to make it happen? How will you know if it has had successful impact?

Practice tasks

Plan for forgetting	Revisit threshold concepts	Knowledge organisers
• Think about topics you have already taught and make a list. • In these topics, note down what are the most important pieces of knowledge you need students to remember. • Devise a revision list to cover these topics and create short quizzes to test whether the students have revised these past topics.	• Think about a topic you are going to teach next. • Break down the topic into the most important threshold concepts that students need to master. • Decide how you are going to teach these threshold concepts at least three times over the course of the topic.	• Think about the key pieces of knowledge you want students to remember about a topic you have taught. • Design a one-page exemplar for students to see how to create a knowledge organiser. • Then decide on the knowledge organisers you want students to make as a revision tool.

Reflection and evaluation of the session

Reflection and evaluation

Question	Response
What strategies do you already routinely use with students to improve students' memories?	
What did you want to get out of today's session?	
How has today's session developed your understanding of how to improve retention in your students' memories?	
What specific changes are you going to commit to making after today's session?	
What further information or training would you like the lead learner to offer to support you in achieving these changes?	

Twilight 4 planning document: Increasing students' commitment to learning

Focus	Timing	Content
Set the tone and share aims of the session	5 minutes	• Start off the training by sharing the session plan and aims. • Ask participants if there are any other aims they would like to add. • Participants share their thoughts on the attributes of a committed learner.
Wider reading task based on summaries of key educational thinkers' research	10 minutes	• Put participants into groups of four to investigate the research of key educational thinkers from chapter 4: one from each group is allocated Ron Berger (page 60), John Hattie (page 66), Carol Dweck (page 64) and Gordon Stobart (page 74). • Each participant is given a handout to read about their educational thinker (from online) and they highlight the key ideas. • Participants share the key ideas with the rest of their group.
Discussion on different ideas from the key educational thinkers relating back to own school context	10 minutes	• Display the debate questions on PowerPoint slide 5. • Participants discuss in their groups the ideas of Berger, Hattie, Dweck and Stobart, linking them to their own student context.
Introduce specific strategies based on research of key educational thinkers	10 minutes	• Display the practical strategies based on the research of Berger, Hattie, Dweck and Stobart (see also chapter 4, page 57): Berger – Redrafting process; Hattie – Help desk; Dweck – Student learning audit; Stobart – Learning wall. • For each strategy, display the thinking prompts that follow for consideration by the participants.
Coaching conversations on possible strategies to try out for own class context	15 minutes	• Show the participants the GROW model of coaching with suggested questions to use as conversation prompts. • Split the groups of four into two pairs. In these pairs, each participant coaches their partner through a particular strategy they could use to encourage greater commitment to learning from their students.

Stretch and Challenge

Focus	Timing	Content
Practice task focusing on applying these strategies	15 minutes	• Introduce the practice tasks. • Participants select the strategy that they think will be most useful for developing the level of challenge with a particular class or group of students following their coaching conversation, and complete the practice task.
Reflection and evaluation of the session	10 minutes	• Return to the aims of the session and remind participants what the session has set out to achieve. • Participants select a potential class or group of students to trial the strategy with. However, no final decisions will be made until all four sessions have been attended. • Hand out evaluation forms to participants so that they reflect and evaluate their knowledge and set their next steps to increase students' commitment to learning.

PowerPoint slides: Twilight 4: Increasing students' commitment to learning

Set the tone and share aims of the session

Aims of the session

1. To engage with the ideas of John Hattie, Ron Berger, Carol Dweck and Gordon Stobart about how to challenge students.
2. To share effective strategies based on research about attitudes to learning and fostering resilience.
3. To reflect on how to implement these strategies with our own classes.
4. To modify existing practice to improve the outcomes of a particular class or a targeted group of students.

Why is student attitude to learning vital for success?

How would you identify if a student is committed to learning?

What impact does having a positive attitude to learning have on what a student can achieve?

Take a couple of minutes to discuss these questions with the person sitting next to you.

Discussion on different ideas from the key educational thinkers relating back to own school context

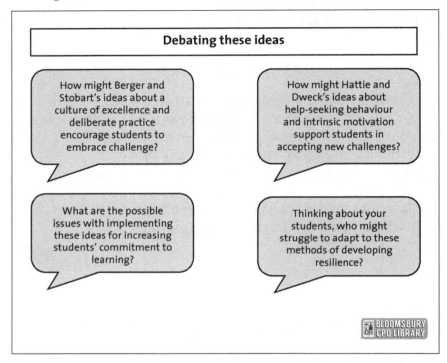

Debating these ideas

How might Berger and Stobart's ideas about a culture of excellence and deliberate practice encourage students to embrace challenge?

How might Hattie and Dweck's ideas about help-seeking behaviour and intrinsic motivation support students in accepting new challenges?

What are the possible issues with implementing these ideas for increasing students' commitment to learning?

Thinking about your students, who might struggle to adapt to these methods of developing resilience?

Introduce specific strategies based on research of key educational thinkers

Implementing Berger's ideas

Practical strategy: Redrafting process

- Give students the opportunity to redraft their work based on your feedback before they hand in their finished piece.
- Even work that meets all of the criteria can be refined if given helpful feedback.
- Encourage students to hand in the first and final draft of their work to make visible how they have improved their work based on feedback.
- You may even want your students to annotate their work to say exactly what they have focused on to make their work better.

Implementing Hattie's ideas

Practical strategy: Help desk

- Encourage your students to become help-seeking rather than too dependent on you or a particular resource, by setting up a help desk in your classroom with a range of resources that might be useful to students.
- Before starting a task, students discuss what they will need to do to be successful and what they might find difficult.
- Set all students off without any help and create windows of time when students can visit the help desk if they feel they need extra support.
- Once they have finished their piece of work, get the students to write a commentary about what help they made use of so they get into the habit of being responsible for their own learning.

Implementing Dweck's ideas

Practical strategy: Student learning audit

- Create an audit of skills and knowledge you would like your students to have mastered.
- Students complete an audit at the beginning of the topic.
- Schedule one-to-one time throughout the topic with those students who you feel need to develop particular skills.
- Talk with them about how they could show themselves and you how they are actively trying to develop particular skills.
- During the unit, students can refer back to their audit and see where they are making improvements.

Implementing Stobart's ideas

Practical strategy: Learning wall

- Create a whole-class learning wall or have a template for each student to support students in understanding how all the different pieces of learning fit together into a bigger picture throughout a topic.
- After each lesson, the students can add 'bricks' to their wall, making connections between the various learning objectives.
- Towards the end of the topic before the final assessment, students can look at their learning wall and decide areas they are least confident about.
- The teacher then sets up specific deliberate practice tasks for groups of students working on the same area of improvement.

Our students

> Take a minute to think about a student, a group of students or a class you teach who might benefit from this strategy.
>
> Why have you chosen these particular students?
>
> Be ready to share your selected students with the rest of the group.

Practice task focusing on applying these strategies

The GROW model – increasing students' commitment to learning

GOAL	REALITY	OPTIONS	WAY FORWARD
Which strategy do you want to try out? Which students might benefit? How might these students benefit from this strategy?	What barriers to learning are you encountering from these students? How are these barriers affecting their ability to think deeply about ideas discussed in your class?	What have you tried already? What were the pros and cons to what you've tried? How might this strategy be better?	What actions are you going to commit to moving forward? What support will you need to make it happen? How will you know if it has had successful impact?

Practice tasks

Redrafting process	Help desk	Student learning audit	Learning wall
• Think about a topic you are going to teach. • Note down the key knowledge and skills you would cover in this topic. • Create one formal assessment which covers the key knowledge and skills and tweak the current scheme of work to allow for students to work on multiple drafts of the same assessment.	• Think about a topic you are going to teach. • Note down what new information you would share with students. • Decide on a list of resources that students could access to find out this information. • Write a clear set of task instructions to allow students to work independently but use the help desk.	• Think about a topic you are going to teach soon. • In this topic, decide on the key knowledge and skills you are going to cover. • Create a learning audit where students judge their own knowledge and skills and which you can use to work with them to explicitly develop particular areas of learning.	• Think about a topic you are going to teach next. • Break down the topic into a series of learning objectives. • Devise the template for the learning wall. • Then once you have all your 'bricks', note down deliberate practice tasks for each brick that students could work on to improve their learning.

Reflection and evaluation of the session

Reflection and evaluation

Question	Response
What strategies do you already routinely use with students to encourage greater commitment to learning?	
What did you want to get out of today's session?	
How has today's session developed your understanding of how to support students to embrace challenge?	
What specific changes are you going to commit to making after today's session?	
What further information or training would you like the lead learner to offer to support you in achieving these changes?	

Lesson study sessions

This training programme includes six lesson study sessions:

1. Deciding on the enquiry question and getting to grips with the big ideas
2. Planning the first lesson in light of research
3. Reflecting on the first lesson and refining the strategies for the second lesson
4. Reflecting on the second lesson and engaging with further research for the third lesson
5. Reflecting on the third lesson and evaluating the success of the strategies implemented
6. Public presentations of lesson study projects

These six sessions would run over **at least** two terms because observations, student interviews and follow-up conversations need to take place between each session. Each session is led by the department's lead learner, and the lesson study pairs and trios remain the same throughout the project. It is imperative that once the pairs or trios have been decided there be no changes. The groups need to stay the same so that each teacher is able to build a clear narrative about the progress the targeted students are making after each visit they make to their colleagues' classes.

Planning overview

Focus	Notes
Facilitators	• Each lesson study session will be delivered by a lead learner from each department who has been identified as an excellent practitioner and who is able to communicate effectively with the rest of the team. • The lead learner will have carried out extensive reading around stretch and challenge and will be able to share this knowledge and support with teachers in selecting appropriate strategies to try with their students.
Session aims	Each session has the same aims but the content of the session is different. 1. To engage with the ideas of key educational thinkers linked to the focus area of stretch and challenge. 2. To share effective strategies based on research. 3. To reflect on how to implement these strategies with our own classes. 4. To modify existing practice to improve the outcomes of a particular class or a targeted group of students.

Focus	Notes
Preparation tasks	• Email staff a week in advance to remind them that the session is running and inform them of anything they will need to bring with them. • Liaise with the department lead learners who are running the lesson study sessions to check there are no issues with their session outline and resources. • Print off wider reading handouts for each session. • Print off lesson study documents: planning learning form, observing learning form, student feedback form and final report template.
Resources required	• PowerPoint presentations. • Wider reading for each session. • Case study scenarios. • Audio equipment and connection to the Internet. • Lesson study documents. • Evaluation forms.
Follow-up commitment	• After each lesson study session, teachers will commit to delivering the planned lesson, be observed by their peers and receive feedback about the reaction of targeted students to the strategy being used before the next lesson study session.
Possible problems and solutions	**Problem:** Lesson study is a big commitment if it is done well. Staff will need to engage with research to make the project purposeful. They will also need to manage their time well to ensure they carry out all of the tasks required of them before the next lesson study session. **Solution:** The CPD leader must negotiate with the headteacher to agree cover requirements in advance; this whole-school programme cannot run unless an agreed amount of cover is given to staff to complete their observations. The lesson study sessions and the window for each observation cycle must be timetabled on the school calendar.

Session 1 planning document: Deciding on the enquiry question and getting to grips with the big ideas

Focus	Timing	Content
Share the lesson study process and the aims of the session	15 minutes	• Start off the training by sharing the session plan and aims. • Ask participants if there are any other aims they would like to add. • Show the lesson study diagram to participants. • Discuss as a whole group why this model could be effective in improving student outcomes.
Reading task based on research	15 minutes	• Put participants into groups of two or three, according to the number of participants. Ask each group to investigate the research of one of the educational thinkers from chapter 4 (page 57) by reading the handout (from online). • Each group reads about their educational thinker and highlights the key ideas. • Each group feeds back their ideas to the other groups so all participants have a good understanding of all the educational thinkers.
Discussion on different ideas from the research relating back to own school context	10 minutes	• Debate the questions on PowerPoint slide 5 and link them to your own student context. • Participants discuss which educational research they would like to engage with during the lesson study programme. • Participants are put into groups of two or three based on what they have said they would like to engage with during the programme.
Introduce case study scenarios to model the process of selecting a strategy to try out with targeted students	15 minutes	• Share the following case study scenarios from chapter 5: scenario 2 – a coasting top set (page 88) and scenario 5 – a group of learners with low levels of literacy in a mixed ability class (page 95). Explain that these two scenarios have been selected as they show how low-achieving and high-achieving students can benefit from being the focus of a lesson study programme. • In their lesson study groups of two or three, participants discuss which of the approaches identified in the case studies may be useful to removing the students' barriers to learning in the case study.

Focus	Timing	Content
		• Show the participants the full stretch and challenge intervention cycle (page 85), and discuss the pros and cons to the strategies selected in the case studies. At this point, make clear that lesson study is a process of trial and error and as the programme continues, participants will make tweaks to the strategies they are trialling.
Deciding on the enquiry question and baseline test	10 minutes	• Participants work in pairs or trios to establish the group's enquiry question for the lesson study project. Everyone in the group will have the same focus but their chosen students will be different as they will pick three students from their own class to trial the strategies with during the course of the lesson study programme. These students will be referred to as Students A, B and C on lesson study records throughout the programme. • Participants then decide on individual baseline tests they are going to carry out before they begin their lesson study project to ensure they have reliable data to analyse at the end of the project.
Reflection and evaluation of the session	10 minutes	• Return to the aims of the session and remind participants what the session has set out to achieve. • Remind the participants of the follow-up actions required before the next lesson study session: to carry out the baseline test and to read one further piece of research linked to the chosen stretch and challenge focus.

PowerPoint slides: Lesson study session 1 – deciding on the enquiry question and getting to grips with the big ideas

Share the lesson study process and the aims of the session

Aims of the session

1. To understand the process of lesson study.
2. To engage with research focusing on stretching and challenging students.
3. To identify strategies to implement with targeted students.
4. To decide on an enquiry question.
5. To decide on the baseline test before starting lesson study.

Discussion on different ideas from the research relating back to own school context

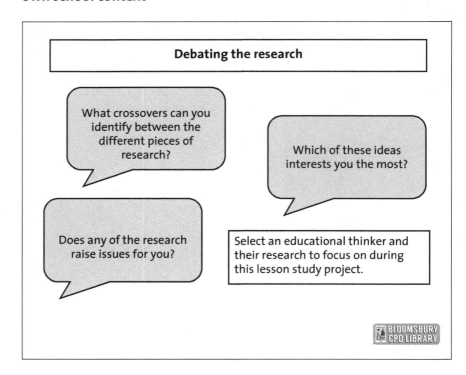

Deciding on the enquiry question and baseline test

Deciding on the enquiry question

Will peer support help my students become more independent?	**Will peer support through feedback improve the quality of students' writing?**
• This is not a good enquiry question as it is too broad and it will be difficult to measure impact.	• This is a better question as the focus is narrower and you can identify impact through the students' writing.

Deciding on the baseline test

	Ideas for a baseline test
• You will need to create a baseline test before beginning lesson study.	
	• A piece of writing
	• Reading comprehension
• This baseline test needs to establish what the students know and can do before you test out your new strategies.	• A verbal presentation
	• A test with a series of questions
	• A performance
	• A physical product

Reflection and evaluation of the session

Reflection and evaluation

Our aims

- To understand the process of lesson study.
- To engage with research focusing on stretching and challenging students.
- To identify strategies to implement with targeted students.
- To decide on an enquiry question.
- To decide on the baseline test before starting lesson study.

Follow-up actions

1. To carry out your baseline test
2. To read a further piece of research

Session 2 planning document: Planning the first lesson in light of research

Focus	Timing	Content
Share the aims of the session and reflect on actions from the previous session	15 minutes	• Share the aims of the session. • Show the lesson study diagram (page 228) to participants to remind them of what stage they're at now. • In their lesson study groups, participants discuss the findings of their base line test on the three students in the class they have selected for data collection.
Discussion in pairs or trios sharing the piece of research they have read in-between sessions	15 minutes	• Staying in their lesson study groups, participants summarise key ideas of the research they read before the session. • Participants discuss how these new readings might influence the direction of their lesson study project.
Modelling how to co-plan the first lesson	10 minutes	• Watch the video clip of an example literacy lesson study lesson planning session. • Based on the video, the participants discuss as a whole group the potential benefits of co-planning compared to traditional lesson planning.
Co-planning the first lesson	25 minutes	• Hand out the planning record to participants (available online). • Participants collaborate in their lesson study groups to plan a lesson that they will each teach featuring their selected strategies included in their enquiry question. Each member of the lesson study group will have a copy of the planning record when they observe the targeted students in their colleagues' classes.
Reflection and evaluation of the session	10 minutes	• Return to the aims of the session and remind participants what the session has set out to achieve. • Hand out the two forms participants will need when observing their colleagues: Observing learning record 1 and Student discussion record. • Discuss the follow-up actions required by each participant before the next lesson study session: to deliver the lesson they co-planned in their lesson study group; to observe another member of their lesson study group delivering the co-planned lesson and to complete the Observing learning record 1 form; to interview the targeted students in the observed lesson and complete the student discussion record.

PowerPoint slides: Lesson study session 2 – planning the first lesson in light of research

Share the aims of the session and reflect on actions from the previous session

---

Aims of the session

1. To reflect on the findings of our baseline test data.
2. To engage with further research on particular strategies chosen in the previous session.
3. To carry out joint planning for the first cycle of lesson study.

Baseline test data

What does your baseline data show?

- Are there any patterns?
- Are there any surprises?
- Are the strategies you've chosen still appropriate or do you need to tweak your focus?

Discussion in pairs or trios sharing the piece of research they have read in-between sessions

---

Engaging with further research

What have you read since the last session?

- What were the key ideas?
- Did they complement or conflict with what you've read previously?
- How might you bring this research into your planning?

Please share your thoughts to these questions with your lesson study group.

BLOOMSBURY CPD LIBRARY

Co-planning the first lesson

How to carry out lesson study planning

Watch this video clip showing three teachers who are beginning to plan their first lesson focusing on improving targeted students' writing, in particular their sentence construction.
www.youtube.com/
watch?v=6yyFsp6vIzU

> What are the benefits of joint planning?

> What do you notice is different about this way of planning compared to traditional lesson planning?

BLOOMSBURY CPD LIBRARY

Planning record 1					
Enquiry question					
Focus strategies		**How specifically will you implement these strategies in this lesson to challenge students?**			
What can Student A do comfortably?	What might Student A do once they are challenged?	What can Student B do comfortably?	What might Student B do once they are challenged?	What can Student C do comfortably?	What might Student C do once they are challenged?

Reflection and evaluation of the session

Reflection and evaluation	
Our aims	**Follow-up actions**
• To reflect on the findings of our baseline test data. • To engage with further research on particular strategies chosen in the previous session. • To carry out joint planning for the first cycle of lesson study.	1. To arrange your lesson study observation 2. To observe a colleague and interview targeted students

Observing learning record 1
Enquiry question

Does Student A respond to the new strategies as predicted?	Does Student B respond to the new strategies as predicted?	Does Student C respond to the new strategies as predicted?

BLOOMSBURY
CPD LIBRARY

Student discussion record 1			
	Student A	Student B	Student C
What parts of the lesson did you find a challenge where you had to push yourself to do well?			
What did your teacher do or say during the lesson that helped you to tackle this challenging learning?			
If your teacher was going to teach that lesson again, what would you have liked them to do to support you further?			

Session 3 planning document: Reflecting on the first lesson and refining the strategies for the second lesson

Focus	Timing	Content
Share the aims of the session	5 minutes	• Share the aims of the session. • Show the lesson study diagram to participants to point out what stage they're at now.
Modelling how to discuss the first lesson findings	15 minutes	• Watch the video clip of an example literacy lesson study post-lesson discussion. • Based on the video, the participants discuss how this type of discussion is useful in challenging students further in the next lesson.
Discussion in pairs or trios exploring what impact the chosen strategies had on the targeted students	20 minutes	• Participants collaborate in their lesson study groups and summarise the reactions of the targeted students to the chosen strategies, using their completed observing learning record and student discussion record to scaffold the discussion.
Co-planning the second lesson	25 minutes	• Hand out the second Planning record to participants (available online). • Participants collaborate in their lesson study groups to plan a second lesson featuring their selected strategies included in their enquiry question.
Reflection and evaluation of the session	10 minutes	• Return to the aims of the session and remind participants what the session has set out to achieve. • Hand out the two forms participants will need when observing their colleagues: Observing learning record 2 and Student discussion record. • Discuss the follow-up actions required by each participant before the next lesson study session: to deliver the second lesson and be observed by a member of their lesson study group; to observe another member of their lesson study group and complete the Observing learning record 2; to interview the targeted students in the observed lesson and complete the student discussion record.

PowerPoint slides: Lesson study session 3 – Reflecting on the first lesson and refining the strategies for the second lesson

Share the aims of the session and reflect on actions from the previous session

---

Aims of the session

1. To reflect on the findings from the first lesson study observation and student interview.
2. To explore possible tweaks to practice based on these findings.
3. To carry out joint planning for the second cycle of lesson study.

Modelling how to discuss the first lesson findings

How to reflect on the first lesson

Watch this video clip showing three teachers who are reflecting on how the students responded to the first lesson they planned.

www.youtube.com/watch?v=u1_ow7l56jQ

What are the benefits of joint planning?

What do you notice is different about this way of planning compared to traditional lesson planning?

Discussion in pairs or trios exploring what impact the chosen strategies had on the targeted students

Reflecting on the first lesson

How did the students respond during the lesson and what feedback did they give the observer?

- Did all of the students respond positively to the new way of being challenged?
- Were there any surprises?
- Are the strategies you've chosen still appropriate or do you need to tweak your use of them in light of this first lesson?

Co-planning the second lesson

Planning the second lesson

- What is the best way forward now for these students?
- What will you keep the same?
- What will you do differently?

Please spend time planning the second lesson.

Planning record 2

Enquiry question

Focus strategies		How specifically will you implement these strategies in this lesson to challenge students?			
What can Student A do comfortably?	What might Student A do once they are challenged?	What can Student B do comfortably?	What might Student B do once they are challenged?	What can Student C do comfortably?	What might Student C do once they are challenged?

Reflection and evaluation of the session

Reflection and evaluation

Our aims
- To reflect on the findings from the first lesson study observation and student interview.
- To explore possible tweaks to practice based on these findings.
- To carry out joint planning for the second cycle of lesson study.

Follow up actions
1. To arrange your second lesson study observation
2. To observe a colleague for the second time and interview targeted students

Observing learning record 2

Enquiry question

Does Student A respond to the new strategies as predicted?	Does Student B respond to the new strategies as predicted?	Does Student C respond to the new strategies as predicted?

BLOOMSBURY CPD LIBRARY

Student discussion record 2			
	Student A	Student B	Student C
What parts of the lesson did you find a challenge where you had to push yourself to do well?			
What did your teacher do or say during the lesson that helped you to tackle this challenging learning?			
If your teacher was going to teach that lesson again, what would you have liked them to do to support you further?			
			BLOOMSBURY CPD LIBRARY

Session 4 planning document: Reflecting on the second lesson and engaging with further research for the third lesson

Focus	Timing	Content
Share the aims of the session	5 minutes	• Share the aims of the session. • Show the lesson study diagram (page 228) to participants pointing out what stage they're at now.
Introduce another case study scenario to model the process of refining and tweaking a strategy being trialled with targeted students	15 minutes	• Share the following case study scenario from chapter 5: scenario 4 –a disengaged, low-achieving group of students (page 93). Explain that you are sharing another case study to use as a stimulus for discussing how strategies selected at the start of lesson study will now need to be refined and tweaked following data from observing learning and student discussion records indicating how students are responding to the strategies. • Remind the participants of the full stretch and challenge intervention cycle (page 85), and focus on the final part of the cycle: tweak.
Discussion in pairs or trios exploring what impact the chosen strategies had on the targeted students	20 minutes	• Working in their lesson study groups, participants summarise the reactions of the targeted students to their chosen strategies, using the observing learning record and student discussion record to scaffold the discussion. • Participants discuss in their groups further tweaks to the strategies they are using based on the information they have from their records so far.
Co-planning the third lesson	25 minutes	• Hand out the third Planning record to participants (available online). • Participants collaborate in their lesson study groups to plan a third lesson featuring their selected strategies included in their enquiry question.
Reflection and evaluation of the session	10 minutes	• Return to the aims of the session and remind participants what the session has set out to achieve. • Hand out the two forms participants will need when observing their colleagues: Observing learning record 3 and Student discussion record. • Discuss the follow-up actions required by each participant before the next lesson study session: to deliver the third lesson and be observed by a member of their lesson study group; to observe another member of their lesson study group and complete the Observing learning record 3; to interview the targeted students in the observed lesson and complete the student discussion record.

PowerPoint slides: Lesson study session 4 – Reflecting on the second lesson and engaging with further research for the third lesson

Share the aims of the session

Aims of the session

1. To compare the response of the students from the first lesson to the second lesson.
2. To consider how to tweak your approach for the final lesson.
3. To carry out joint planning for the third cycle of lesson study.

Discussion in pairs or trios exploring what impact the chosen strategies had on the targeted students

---

Reflecting on the second lesson

How did the students respond during the second lesson in comparison to the first lesson?

- Did students respond more positively?
- Were students able to complete more challenging work in comparison to the first lesson?
- Are the strategies you've chosen still appropriate or do you need to tweak your use of them in light of this second lesson?

Co-planning the third lesson

Planning the third lesson

- Are you starting to notice changes in the targeted students?
- What will you keep the same?
- What will you do differently?

Please spend time planning the third lesson.

Planning record 3

Enquiry question

Focus strategies		How specifically will you implement these strategies in this lesson to challenge students?			
What can Student A do comfortably?	What might Student A do once they are challenged?	What can Student B do comfortably?	What might Student B do once they are challenged?	What can Student C do comfortably?	What might Student C do once they are challenged?

Reflection and evaluation of the session

Reflection and evaluation

Our aims

1. To compare the response of the students from the first lesson to the second lesson.
2. To consider how to tweak your approach for the final lesson.
3. To carry out joint planning for the third cycle of lesson study.

Follow-up actions

1. To arrange your third lesson study observation
2. To observe a colleague for the third time and interview targeted students

Observing learning record 3

Enquiry question

Does Student A respond to the new strategies as predicted?	Does Student B respond to the new strategies as predicted?	Does Student C respond to the new strategies as predicted?

Student discussion record 3

	Student A	Student B	Student C
What parts of the lesson did you find a challenge where you had to push yourself to do well?			
What did your teacher do or say during the lesson that helped you to tackle this challenging learning?			
If your teacher was going to teach that lesson again, what would you have liked them to do to support you further?			

BLOOMSBURY
CPD LIBRARY

Session 5 planning document: Reflecting on the third lesson and evaluating the success of the strategies implemented

Focus	Timing	Content
Share the aims of the session	5 minutes	• Share the aims of the session. • Show the lesson study diagram (page 228) to participants pointing out what stage they're at now.
Discussion in pairs or trios exploring what impact the chosen strategies had on the targeted students	20 minutes	• Working in their lesson study groups, participants summarise the reactions of the targeted students to their chosen strategies, using the observing learning record and student discussion record to scaffold the discussion.
Read about measuring impact of a lesson study project	20 minutes	• Read Stephen Tierney's blog about judging the impact of a lesson study project. • Working in their lesson study groups, participants summarise the impact of their lesson study project, referring back to the baseline test and the latest assessment data.
Preparing for the lesson study report	20 minutes	• Distribute copies of the lesson study report handout (from online). • Lead the participants through the questions and take questions about completing the report. • Tell participants that the lesson study report will be used as the basis of their presentation in the final session. They will present as a group on using the questions in the lesson study report as subheadings for their presentation. Each group's presentation will be 15 minutes. • Tell lesson study groups they must include audio and/or visual stimuli to help the audience understand the progress the targeted students have made during lesson study. Examples of stimuli might be: excerpts from students' exercise books; copies of tests; videos of students working in class; audio recordings of students' discussions.
Reflection and evaluation of the session	10 minutes	• Return to the aims of the session and remind participants what the session has set out to achieve. • Discuss the follow-up actions required by each participant before the next lesson study session: to write up their lesson study report and prepare their presentation using visual and/or audio stimuli.

PowerPoints Session 5: Reflecting on the third lesson and evaluating the success of the strategies implemented

Share the aims of the session

Aims of the session

1. To reflect on the changes in the targeted students after three cycles of lesson study.
2. To consider the impact of the strategies used based on the final assessment.
3. To begin preparing the lesson study report to present in the final session.

Discussion in pairs or trios exploring what impact the chosen strategies had on the targeted students

---

Reflecting on the third lesson

How did the students respond during the third lesson in comparison to the first and second lessons?

- Can you see a noticeable difference in the way students are learning?
- Which strategies have had the most impact?

Read about measuring impact of a lesson study project

Measuring impact

- Read this blog post by Stephen Tierney about his school's use of lesson study.
- leadinglearner.me/2014/06/07/lesson-study-3-heads-are-better-than-1
- As you read the post, consider the difference between your baseline test and the final assessment to show what impact the strategies have had on students.
- If there hasn't been a positive impact for all of the targeted students, why might this be and how could you address this in future planning?

Preparing for the lesson study report

Lesson study report

- What was your enquiry question?
- Who were your targeted students and why?
- Can you summarise in 250 words the specific research you engaged with?
- What did the baseline test tell you about the students?
- Based on the three lessons, can you explain the changes you saw in Student A?
- Based on the three lessons, can you explain the changes you saw in Student B?
- Based on the three lessons, can you explain the changes you saw in Student C?
- What did the final assessment tell you about the impact of the chosen strategies?
- How will you move forward in your approach to stretch and challenge now you have completed this lesson study project?

Reflection and evaluation of the session

Reflection and evaluation

Our aims

1. To reflect on the changes in the targeted students after three cycles of lesson study.
2. To consider the impact of the strategies used based on the final assessment.
3. To begin preparing the lesson study report to present in the final session.

Follow-up actions

1. To complete your lesson study report
2. To create your presentation for the group to include audio and/ or visual materials.

Session 6 planning document: Public presentations of lesson study projects

Focus	Timing	Content
Share the aims of the session and reflect on actions from the previous session	5 minutes	• Share the aims of the session. • Show the lesson study diagram (page 228) to participants pointing out what stage they're at now.
Presentations of lesson study projects	1 hour	• Each lesson study group presents their findings using the subheadings from the lesson study report • After each presentation, participants from other groups and the lead learner have an opportunity to ask questions based on the presentation. These questions could focus on the lesson study process, examples of research referred to, any surprising results, or next steps for continuing with the chosen strategies.
Reflection and evaluation of lesson study	10 minutes	• Participants are asked to share their top tips for participating in lesson study now they have completed their first lesson study programme. • The lead learner summarises the key findings from the presentations and collates these for the whole group and to share with the whole school.

PowerPoints Session 6: Public presentations of lesson study projects

Share the aims of the session

> # Aims of the session
>
> 1. To listen to the achievements of our colleagues.
> 2. To reflect on which strategies as a group have had most impact on our students.
> 3. To consider how the findings from the lesson study projects can be shared with the whole school.
>
>

Presentations of lesson study projects

> # Presenting your lesson study projects
>
> - Each group is now going to present their lesson study projects.
>
> - The groups will address the questions from the lesson study report but will include audio or visual materials to help us understand the journey from baseline test to final assessment.
>
> - Please listen to the presentations carefully as there will be an opportunity to ask questions to the groups once they have delivered their presentations.
>
>

Reflection and evaluation of lesson study

Reflection and evaluation

What would be your top tips for someone who is thinking of starting lesson study?

What are the most effective strategies from the whole group that we need to share with the rest of the school?

BLOOMSBURY
CPD LIBRARY

3 Evaluation and next steps

Congratulations! You have now got to the final chapter of the book and it's a good time to take stock of all that you have achieved. At this point, you should be feeling confident about your own expertise in providing high-quality, challenging learning experiences for your students. You have engaged with the research of some of the key educational thinkers and applied this to your own classroom context. Your new approach to stretch and challenge and your use of well-researched strategies should have led to improved achievement for your students.

As well as improving your own practice, you've also supported the training of others if you have used Part 2 of this book. If you have taken the lead in delivering training then you will want to know the impact the training has had across your school as we are always looking to improve our own and others' practice. Getting better at providing high-quality stretch and challenge for your students takes continuous effort; as the students respond to higher levels of challenge, you will need to rethink what they will need from you to keep them on a journey of progression. At a whole-school level, all teachers will need to work together to embed the vision of stretch and challenge across school so that students embrace the idea of being constantly challenged to develop their learning.

Evaluating the success of the Stretch and Challenge CPD

Here is a form that you could use as a CPD leader to evaluate the impact of your stretch and challenge CPD programme. It is important as a CPD leader to evaluate the training that staff receive as you will want to consider the successes of the training, identify aspects of the training that could be improved and what gaps there still are in teachers' knowledge.

Evaluating the whole-school CPD programme	
In answering these questions, consider what evidence you are drawing upon to comment on impact.	
What were your top priorities for stretch and challenge and why were these your priorities?	
What opportunities have there been for individual teachers to develop their practice?	

What opportunities have there been for departments to develop their practice?	
What shifts in attitude have you identified in school culture regarding stretch and challenge?	
Which members of staff have you identified who can be used to spread the successes of the CPD?	
What changes will you need to make to CPD so that high-quality stretch and challenge is embedded into the teaching and learning routines of the school?	

Fig. 24 CPD leader form – evaluating whole-school CPD

As well as the CPD leader evaluating the impact of the stretch and challenge CPD programme, the lead learners and middle leaders who make a significant contribution to CPD delivery should complete an evaluation. Their role should be to communicate to the CPD leader the strengths and areas for development of the participants whom they have been working with during the CPD. Here is a form that those who are responsible for delivering training could use and share with their CPD leader.

Evaluating the training sessions	
In answering these questions, consider what evidence you are drawing upon to comment on impact.	
What were your aims for the sessions you delivered and why were these aims important for developing staff practice?	
What 'bright spots' have you seen during your sessions where participants have developed their stretch and practice provision?	

Which participants would benefit from more intensive support to ensure their stretch and challenge provision is enabling students to achieve well?	
What changes would you suggest to the training you delivered if you were to deliver the training again to other participants?	

Fig. 25 Lead learner form – evaluating training sessions

In order for CPD leaders or lead learners to evaluate the impact of any CPD opportunities provided for staff, they will need to consider what form of evidence they are going to use to make their judgements. No one type of evidence is going to show you everything you need to know about whether teachers' practice is having impact on their students' achievement; you will need to select a range of evidence to make an informed judgement.

Evidence type	What information will you be able to find out?	What are the issues to consider when using this evidence?
Student work scrutiny	• The type of tasks students are completing • The quality of work produced • The different levels of challenge in a task • The quality of teacher feedback • Students responding to teacher feedback to close learning gaps	• Sometimes written work does not accurately reflect what students have learnt if there is a specific learning need linked to writing.
Student learning forum	• Students' awareness of teachers' approaches to stretch and challenge • Students' understanding of their own strengths and weaknesses • Students' response to teachers trialling new strategies and approaches to stretch and challenge • Students' attitudes to being challenged by their teachers	• Student interviews are time consuming and you cannot interview every student so ensure your sample is fair if you are looking to get a whole-school picture.

Evidence type	What information will you be able to find out?	What are the issues to consider when using this evidence?
Student survey	• Students' awareness of teachers' approaches to stretch and challenge • Students' understanding of their own strengths and weaknesses • Students' response to teachers trialling new strategies and approaches to stretch and challenge • Students' attitudes to being challenged by their teachers	• This is an easier and quicker way to get feedback from a large group of students but you will need to think carefully about the wording of the questions to ensure they are easy to comprehend and do not lead to any kind of bias.
Teacher CPD report	• Teachers' goals for improvement • Teachers' engagement with research • Teachers' use of data to diagnose students' learning barriers • Teachers' trialling of new strategies and approaches with students	• The teacher may not be able to evidence impact of all the strategies if the report only allows hard data to be included. Sometimes softer data can capture a more holistic view of student learning.
Schemes of work review	• Quality of resources • Clear progression in learning across the lessons • Rich and diverse tasks that all students can access and engage with to increase their achievement • Challenging learning intentions for the scheme of work • Useful and challenging homework opportunities	• Although it is easy to see how teachers are adapting their planning in light of what they have learnt about stretch and challenge, there is no way to discern how the curriculum has been enacted by teachers.
Learning walks	• Teachers' implementation of new stretch and challenge strategies and approaches • Students' reaction to new stretch and challenge strategies and approaches	• Many teachers feel uncomfortable being observed even in informal settings, which could skew their behaviour. Also observers must be cautious not to suffer from confirmation bias.

Evidence type	What information will you be able to find out?	What are the issues to consider when using this evidence?
Student shadowing	• Teachers' interactions with students • Quality of learning experience across the curriculum • Difference in students' attitudes in different lessons • Students' responses to tasks set in different areas	• Students may feel uncomfortable being watched over an extended period of time and behave differently under scrutiny; make sure students are clear as to why the student shadowing is taking place.
Exam results / progress data	• Students' ability to draw upon their learning and apply their knowledge in test conditions • Teachers' ability to offer appropriate levels of challenge for all students in their class	• Exam results or progress data from tests do not always accurately reflect what students have learnt because many students suffer from performance anxiety under test conditions; consider a range of formative assessment in addition to get a fuller picture of what students know or can do.

Fig. 26 Different types of evidence to consider when evaluating impact of CPD

Formal review of impact of CPD

It is not unusual for schools to take into consideration teachers' participation and engagement with CPD as part of their annual appraisal. At my school, each teacher is expected to engage with CPD throughout the year and is aware they will need to discuss the relationship between their own improvements in practice and their engagement with CPD at various points across the academic year. This should not be a cause for concern amongst staff as we should be expected to be asked how we are improving if we are having time and money invested in us to develop our practice.

The first step should be the CPD leader collating the information from the evaluation forms at the end of each training session. These were referred to in the Training plans section of Part 2, but here is an example to look at now.

Reflection and evaluation

Question	Response
What strategies do you already routinely use with students to develop the quality of their thinking?	
What did you want to get out of today's session?	
How has today's session developed your understanding of how to develop students' thinking?	
What specific changes are you going to commit to making after today's session?	
What further information or training would you like the lead learner to offer to support you in achieving these changes?	

Once the evaluation forms have been collated, the CPD leader should share this information with the SLT and relevant middle leaders. It is important that those who have a role in appraising a member of staff know what their CPD needs are and what they are working on to try and improve their practice.

The SLT should use this information to identify any patterns in teachers' evaluations and build this into the school development plan. For example, it may arise that many teachers feel that stretching middle-achieving students is a priority with their classes and this could be linked to the school development plan if student data show that middle-achieving students on entry aren't making enough progress in comparison to other student groups. It is vital that senior leaders are transparent with middle leaders about the priority areas for the school as leaders at all levels need to promote a consistent message to staff across the school.

Middle leaders should use information from evaluation forms to gain a clear picture of the strengths and weaknesses of their team and consider how this could affect student achievement in their area. Middle leaders will need to discuss with members of their team what they are trialling and help them to reflect on what impact it may be having on their students. After the middle leader has a clear picture of the strengths and needs of their team, then it is their job to ensure there is ample opportunity on a departmental/phase level for teachers to work together to raise the achievements of their students. This could be done by sharing student work, refining current schemes of work or setting up peer observations.

The two formal opportunities for reflection on the impact of CPD are the mid-year review and the final appraisal meeting. In these meetings, it is important that the appraiser speaks openly and honestly with the member of staff, acknowledging where there have been significant developments in practice but also areas the member of staff still needs to work on. In this way, the school will be supporting all teachers to embed their stretch and challenge practice but also recognise that the best teachers are always on a journey of continual self-improvement.

Moving forward to become a beacon of best practice

As all teachers will know, our profession is often guilty of flitting from one new trend to the next and never letting anything embed. We like the novelty of trying new things but it's important to stick at something for at least three years if you want to see substantial change.

At the end of the academic year, it's a good idea for CPD leaders to spend time planning the new CPD programme to ensure that the following year continues to build upon the successes from the year just finished and gives staff a chance to embed their new stretch and challenge approaches and strategies.

The CPD leader should ask themselves the following questions when planning their CPD programme:

What were the successes of this year's CPD programme?

1. How will I adapt the programme to acknowledge the issues raised by staff in their evaluations?
2. Which departments need significant support to become excellent providers of stretch and challenge?
3. Which departments would benefit from greater freedom and choice when deciding which CPD opportunities are most beneficial for them in tweaking their stretch and challenge practice?
4. Which individual teachers have not fully engaged with the whole school CPD programme and what tailored support will they need to develop their stretch and challenge practice?
5. Which members of staff have engaged well and can show positive impact, making them possible candidates to deliver future training to their colleagues?
6. What milestones will be put into the school development plan so that the impact of CPD is measured regularly and any changes made to the programme are timely and responsive to staff needs?

Evaluating current CPD provision and planning future opportunities to develop teachers' stretch and challenge practice takes a lot of time. Remember that you cannot rush a culture shift; yes, you can plan for quick wins but real long-lasting change happens over years rather than months. If you can get staff to buy into the importance of putting stretch and challenge at the heart of teacher development then you will see a significant improvement in students' achievement. After all, what's more important than knowing your students really, really well?

Bibliography and further reading

Alexander, R. (2008a), '*Culture, Dialogue and Learning: Notes on an Emerging Pedagogy*', *Exploring Talk in School, eds. Mercer and Hodkinson, 111.*

Alexander, R. (2008b), *Towards Dialogic Teaching: Rethinking Classroom Talk* (revised 4th edition). York: Dialogos.

Berger, R. (2003), *An Ethic of Excellence: Building a Culture of Craftmanship with Students.* Portsmouth, NH: Heinemann.

Berger, R. (2012), 'Austin's Butterfly: Building Excellence in Student Work' (https://vimeo.com/38247060).

Berger, R. https://www.youtube.com/watch?v=1znB1oxo_EI.

Black, P. and Wiliam, D. (1990), *Inside the Black Box: Raising Standards Through Classroom Assessment.* London: GL Assessment.

Brown, P. C., Roediger, H. L. and McDaniel, M. A. (2014), *Make It Stick: The Science of Successful Learning. Cambridge, MA: Harvard University Press.*

DfE (2011), 'Teachers' Standards'. Crown copyright.

Didau, D. (2014), *The Secret of Literacy: Making the Implicit Explicit.* Carmarthen: Crown House Publishing Ltd.

Dweck, C. (2007), *Mindset: The New Psychology of Success: How We Can Learn to Fulfil our Potential.* New York: Ballantine.

Dweck, C. (2014), 'Developing a Growth Mindset' (www.youtube.com/watch?v=hiiEeMN7vbQ).

Dweck, C. (2014), 'The Growth Mindset' (www.youtube.com/watch?v=whoOS4MrN3E).

Dweck, C. (2014), 'A Study on Praise and Mindsets' (www.youtube.com/watch?v=NWv1VdDeoRY).

Elder, Z. (2012), *Full on Learning: Involve Me and I'll Understand*. Carmarthen: Crown House Publishing Ltd.

Hattie, J. (2012), 'Visible Learning edited highlights Part 2: The Successful Methods' (www.youtube.com/watch?v=TD_yQNk7X3w).

Hattie, J. (2014), 'Challenging All Students' (www.youtube.com/watch?v=Gz-_DyMj2iQ).

Hattie, J. (2015), 'Learning Intentions and Success Criteria' (www.youtube.com/watch?v=dvzeou_u2hM).

Hattie, J. (2015), 'John Hattie on inquiry-based learning' (www.youtube.com/watch?v=YUooOYbgSUg).

Hattie, J. and Yates, G. (2013), *Visible Learning and the Science of How We Learn*. London: Routledge.

Lemov, D. (2015), *Teach Like a Champion 2.0: 62 Techniques that Put Students on the Path to College*. San Francisco: Jossey-Bass.

Lemov, D. (2015), 'Doug Lemov on Teach Like a Champion 2.0' (www.youtube.com/watch?v=1XpWbDjhIiI).

Lemov, D., Woolway, E. and Yezzi, K. (2012), *Practice Perfect: 42 Rules for Getting Better at Getting Better*. San Francisco: Jossey-Bass.

Lessonstudy.uk (2015), 'Literacy Planning: The Lesson Study Video' (www.youtube.com/watch?v=6yyFsp6vIzU).

Lessonstudy.uk (2015), 'Literacy: The Post-Lesson Discussion' (www.youtube.com/watch?v=u1_ow7I56jQ).

Lord, P., Atkinson, M. and Mitchell, H. (2008), *Mentoring and Coaching for Professionals: A Study of the Research Evidence*. London: TDA, p. viii.

Marzano, R. J. and Pickering, D. J. (2005), *Building Academic Vocabulary: Teacher's Manual*. Alexandria, VA: ASCD.

Marzano, R. J. and Simms, J. A. (2013), *Vocabulary for the Common Core*. Bloomington, IN: Marzano Research Laboratory.

Marzano, R. (2013), 'Building Basic Vocabulary with Dr. Robert J. Marzano' (www. youtube.com/watch?v=L_HN09Wos40).

Nuthall, G. (2007), *The Hidden Lives of Learners*. Wellington: NZCER Press.

Petty, G. (2009), *Evidence-Based Teaching: A Practical Approach*. Oxford: Oxford University Press.

Stobart, G. (2014), *The Expert Learner: Challenging the Myth of Ability*. Maidenhead: Open University Press.

Teacher Development Trust (2015), *Developing Great Teaching: Lessons from the International Reviews into Effective Professional Development*. Teacher Development Trust.

Tierney, S. (2014), 'Lesson Study: 3 Heads are Better than 1.' (leadinglearner. me/2014/06/07/lesson-study-3-heads-are-better-than–1).

Wiliam, D. (2011), *Embedded Formative Assessment*. Bloomington, IN: Solution Tree Press.

Wiliam, D. (2012), 'Embedded Formative Assessment' (www.youtube.com/ watch?v=B3HRvFsZHoo).

Wiliam, D. (2012), 'Collaborative Learning' ((https://www.youtube.com/ watch?v=LK_9tWsndEk)).

Wiliam, D. (2015), 'Feedback on Learning' (www.youtube.com/ watch?v=MzDuiqaGqAY).

Willingham, D. T. (2010), *Why Don't Students Like School?: A Cognitive Scientist Answers Questions About How the Mind Works and What It Means for the Classroom*. San Francisco: Jossey-Bass.

Willingham, D. (2008), 'Brain based education: fad or breakthrough' (www. youtube.com/watch?v=vdJ7JWoLgVs).

Useful websites and blogs

Belmont School: belmontteach.wordpress.com

Ron Berger: www.makeitstick.net

Chris Chivers: chrischiversthinks.weebly.com/blog-thinking-aloud.

David Didau: www.learningspy.co.uk

Carol Dweck: www.mindsetonline.com

David Fawcett: reflectionsofmyteaching.blogspot.

Harry Fletcher-Wood: improvingteaching.co.uk

Nancy Gedge: notsoordinarydiary.wordpress.com

John Hattie and Gregory Yates: www.visible-learning.org

Rachel Jones: createinnovateexplore.com

Joe Kirby: https://pragmaticreform.wordpress.com

Doug Lemov: www.teachlikeachampion.com

Robert J. Marzano: www.marzanoresearch.com

Tom Sherrington: www.headguruteacher.com

Andy Tharby: www.reflectingenglish.wordpress.com

Stephen Tierney: leadinglearner.me/2014/06/07/lesson-study-3-headsare-better-than-1

Daniel Willingham: www.danielwillingham.com

Index